THE BEST OF
REMINISCE

CONTENTS

REMINISCE

PICTURED ON FRONT COVER
Soldier in uniform on page 202,
Patrick Murphy

Young couple on page 65,
Gordon Graham

Group of soldiers on page 132,
L.K. Butch Milius

Boy in costume and girl with teddy bear
on page 15, Sharon Sunkle

Louis Armstrong on page 176,
Don Charles

Kids in pajamas on page 39,
Greg Groom

PICTURED ON BACK COVER
Kids in ice skates on page 19,
Mary Lou Decicco

ADDITIONAL PHOTO CREDIT
Vintage scrapbook page,
OHishiapply/Shutterstock

© 2021 RDA Enthusiast Brands, LLC.
1610 N. 2nd St., Suite 102
Milwaukee, WI 53212-3906

International Standard Book Number:
D 978-1-62145-704-6
U 978-1-62145-705-3
Component Number:
D 117300102H
U 117300104H
International Standard Serial Number:
2689-1786

ORCHESTRA SEATING

Once a week for four years I carried my cello on two trolley cars to William Penn High School for Girls in Philadelphia, Pennsylvania, for orchestra practice. In this 1941 picture, I'm the cellist in the white shirt.

NORMA P. BRADLEY · BROOKSVILLE, FL

Our memories of friends, family and milestone events are timeless, much like the music played by the orchestra at left. We hope this keepsake collection of stories and photos from the previous year of *Reminisce* encourages you to reflect on moments in your life that have stood the test of time.

The Best of Reminisce features heartfelt stories of growing up and time spent with family. You'll also find tales of true love, including high school sweethearts who rekindled their romance after 26 years, and read about nostalgic fun, including a humorous night one family spent in a motel.

We've dedicated a chapter to wartime stories from the homefront and soldiers overseas—including one man's harrowing tale of meeting an enemy soldier face to face on the battlefield.

Those with a fondness for pop culture and sports will enjoy readers' chance encounters with celebrities and nostalgic accounts of baseball bringing families together.

We're grateful you've chosen to join us as we remember pieces of the past that made us who we are today. Enjoy.

THE EDITORS OF *REMINISCE* MAGAZINE

CHAPTER 1

GROWING UP

School days, silly fashions and winter fun
bring back fond memories of youth.

A Private Slope

As a kid, I loved sledding in our Willingboro, New Jersey, neighborhood
because we had the place to ourselves. Here I am in 1968 at age 7 with
my brother Blake Anderson, who was 13 at the time.

DEBBIE KOOP · LAKEWOOD, CO

Grandparents Lee and Tony with grandson Joe, holding an ice cream from the American Bar man.

American Bar Man Made Mondays Sweet

Kids kept one ear cocked for the sound of the ice cream truck coming down the street.

——

Every Monday around 3 p.m., some sharp-eared kid would hear bells on the next block and yell, "American Bar is coming!" Kids scrambled in every direction to get a dime, as Gus, the ice cream man, drove his truck onto Clarendon Drive on Long Island, New York.

My dad, Tony, loved ice cream and Monday was his day off. He'd buy ice cream for any kid who didn't have money. Gus knew a good thing when he saw it and parked right in front of our house.

It was the '50s, and Gus, a Greek immigrant, owned his American Bar truck. Painted on the side of the truck were colorful photos of ice cream sandwiches, bars, sundaes and pops, so that little kids who couldn't read could just point.

My mom, Lee, approved of Gus' neatly ironed white pants and starched shirt, black bow tie, and white captain's hat with a black brim. His highly polished black shoes didn't escape her sharp-eyed notice either.

Gus knew everyone's favorite ice cream. He'd try to get me to order something else, but I stuck with vanilla and my sister, Fran, always got a sundae cup. My brother, Joe, got whatever was new and colorful. When I started dating, I was surprised that Gus knew my boyfriend's name. "Joey, what are you doing on this street?" he asked.

Years later, our son, another Joe, got to meet the American Bar man. Gus handed him a vanilla pop: "Your mama's favorite." Joe was impressed—for his fifth birthday, he asked for a change-maker, so he could be like Gus.

JOSEPHINE MELE · MORAGA, CA

Fast Times in Florissant

On his 5-speed Avenger, he was a master of the road.

B ack in 1975 when I was 14, everyone I knew in Florissant, Missouri, had a bicycle. It was the way we got from one place to another before driving a car was even a thought in our minds. Owning a bike opened up a whole new world of adventure.

One year, while flipping through a holiday wish book, I saw an incredible-looking bicycle, the Roadmaster Aerobee Avenger 5 by AMF. It was nearly all chrome with a silver glitter banana seat and handgrips, ape-hanger handlebars, large decaled chain guard, rear racing slick and five-speed gear shift. What a great bike!

I awoke that holiday to see my dream realized—my new bike was under the tree, and because it hadn't yet snowed that Christmas, I was able to try it out right away. This was the first bike I ever had with hand brakes, and the first that could shift gears, allowing me to attain speeds that were never possible with my old fixed-gear bike.

Aside from a racing accident that left me with five stitches in my chin (along with a bruised ego), my memories of the Aerobee Avenger are nothing but amazing, if not magical. Not only was it my favorite of several bikes I later owned, it was the envy of the neighborhood.

I treasure that bike to this day and keep it in good shape. Sometimes I take a ride, as memories of flying down the street, shifting gears and popping wheelies come to mind—and I realize how fortunate I was to have received such a wonderful gift.

NAT TURDO · HAZELWOOD, MO

Nat's dream ride was this Sting-Ray-style Aerobee Avenger from AMF's Roadmaster line of bicycles.

Riding Shotgun on
the New York Central

A young rail fan had a one-track mind.

———

Both my grandpa E.E. Sharp and my dad, Earl, worked for the New York Central Railroad. One of my earliest memories is being in the cab of a steam engine with my grandpa.

We lived close to the South Anderson Yard in Anderson, Indiana. Trains—steam locomotives, in particular—fascinated me.

During the winter, I satisfied my obsession with everything railroad by operating my Lionel train set. On warm summer days, I rode my bike to the railroad yard and parked it in a safe, out-of-the-way

spot. I watched for hours as my grandpa, who was an engineer on the yard engine, made up the trains at the switching yards.

Dad was one of the locomotive engineers. For years, I begged him to take me on a trip with him in the engine, but he didn't think I was old enough. It was in the early '50s, when I was about 12, that he finally determined I'd reached an acceptable age for an overnight trip.

Those were the waning years of railway steam power, and during the transition from steam to diesel, locomotives on the routes from Anderson

Train work ran in the Sharp family. Far left, a fireman and Edward's grandpa drove the yard engine in 1953. Left, Edward and his dad in an engine cab.

Finally, we received the green signal that told us it was safe to slowly leave the yard. I couldn't stop smiling!

used both kinds of energy. The trip north was powered by a diesel engine, and the trip south, to Jeffersonville, was by steam. My trip was to be the route to Jeffersonville and back. The steam locomotive on the trip was a New York Central Mohawk L-4 engine.

On the big day, Dad and I went together to the roundhouse. He did the necessary paperwork, then we climbed aboard the engine. Dad did all the pre-trip checks and adjustments with the fireman, Bob Stierwalt. (Yes, engineers really did walk all through the engine "oiling around.") Next, we hooked up to the train and did the required air checks. Finally, we received the green signal that told us it was safe to slowly leave the yard. I couldn't stop smiling!

The engine was coal fired by a stoker, and I sat on the left side of the cab with Bob and watched his every move. A steam engine is like a living, breathing machine, and maintaining the correct balance of fire and steam pressure, while watching for road signals out the left side, is an art form.

The trip progressed with the usual work of

railroaders everywhere: We went onto a siding to set off and pick up cuts, or sections, of cars. We also made stops to fill the tender with water.

I went back and forth from one side of the cab to the other, watching Dad work the throttle and regulate the air. Every now and then, I was allowed to sound the whistle for a crossing. The highlight of the trip was when, under Bob's supervision, I was allowed to fire the engine for approximately 57 miles, from North Vernon to just before arriving in Jeffersonville. The trip took 10 or 12 hours. We stayed in the bunkhouse overnight and returned to Anderson the next day.

A year later, I got to ride a diesel engine to Elkhart and back on the north route, a trip that was just as intense for me as the Jeffersonville one had been. I never became a railroader myself, although part of me still wishes that I had. Dad died in 1987 and Bob died in the 2010s. I am forever grateful to both men for those wonderful experiences in my life.

EDWARD SHARP · MONTICELLO, IN

The Clothes Make the Nerd

Mom's practical fashion choice was
uncomfortable during the awkward years.

The salesman bragged to my mom, Phoebe, "These jeans are almost indestructible."

Mom and I were shopping for pants, and she was trying to tug the fabric into place around my waist. "They also come in husky sizes," the salesman added. My face turned red.

At 10, I was beginning to notice girls and wanted a cool pair of Levi's. Mom was more partial to Toughskins, Sears' brand of jeans that combined three fabrics for durability and stretch, and were an icon of uncoolness in the 1970s.

I was lucky: Toughskins came in a rainbow of colors, and Mom chose navy. My pants could almost pass for denim. My friend Steve wore Toughskins, too—his were bright red and green, and he even had a plaid pair for special occasions.

We both accessorized with fresh new sneakers from Kmart.

A growing fifth grader, I had a midsection that bloomed over my belt: The space-age fabric blend and industrial construction did not accommodate my growing body. I complained, so Mom stitched thick white elastic into the waistline, forming a contrasting "V" on my backside. Unfortunately, there was nothing she could do about the pants being a little too short.

As my body finally began to stretch out, Mom gave in and took me to the mall for my first pair of Levi's 501 jeans. They say that whatever doesn't kill you makes you stronger. My years in Toughskins certainly made me tougher.

BOB KELSOE · CORONA, CA

FASHION SHOW

» STRIPES AND OVERALLS

My brother Don and I were inseparable growing up in Belle Plaine, Kansas. This picture of us was taken in the 1960s. I still look up to my big brother. Then again, I have to—he's over 6 feet tall.

TAMMY HADER · WICHITA, KS

⌄ ALL IN THE FAMILY

My daughters Sherry, Juanita, Rhonda, Venita and Ramona show off their new autumn clothes at home in 1962.

ROBERTA NADLER · AUGUSTA, MO

FASHION SHOW

AUTUMN IN THE CITY

Here I am with my friend Dorothy Frankowski, left, in front of our apartment house on 43rd Street in Astoria, New York, in 1952. I loved that coat, which was a purple and cream check. I later handed it down to my **sister Charlotte.**
MARYANN HELLDORFER
KINGS PARK, NY

THE WEDDING MARCH

My friend Kathy and I liked to play "bride" in the 1950s. Here we are in some hats and dresses we made.
KATHRYN RIDDER · CHILTON, WI

HOWDY, MA'AM
At 3, I was too young for school in Worthington, Ohio, but my brother, Gary Hazlett, 6, wishes he'd held onto that Hopalong Cassidy lunchbox. Don't you love the cowboy outfit?
SHARON SUNKLE · ESCONDIDO, CA

The Pike amusement park, lower foreground, was a magical spot for Patricia and her brother Ed and sister Peggy during the Great Depression.

LONG BEACH, CALIFORNIA, SHOWING AMUSEMENT ZONE, AUDITORIUM AND RAINBOW PIER 20

Carefree in California

Three siblings make the most of Long Beach life.

My early childhood was spent with my brother Ed, who at 11 was three years older than me, and our sister Peg, 6. Our mother was very busy with our new baby sister, Edith, so in the late 1930s not much attention was paid to three Long Beach kids wandering the streets.

The Pike was one of our favorite hangouts. There were amusement rides, of course, but we liked the indoor pool called the Plunge. It had a balcony, and on occasion our father would walk around the circumference shouting instructions on how to execute the perfect dive: "Point your toes more" or "jump higher before you begin." There was a big fountain in the center of the Plunge where you could sit back as the water came down around you like a curtain.

We had to earn our money for our escapades. My enterprising brother took his shoeshine kit to Lincoln Park, where many adults would agree to a shine—or it could be that they simply took pity on us. Little Peggy was Ed's trump card—who could resist an adorable curly-haired blond girl willing to buff shoes?

When we grew weary of swimming, we went to the arcade, where Ed loved to play pinball, always ignoring the "do not tilt" warnings. Sometimes we'd walk on the beach with a sand sifter and dredge up enough money to go to the movies.

Saturday matinees were 11 cents at the Lee Theatre on Fourth Street. Inside, they'd let us reach into a giant box for a free candy bar.

At home, we played marbles and watched Ed do yo-yo tricks: "walk the dog," "around the world" and "rock the cradle."

He taught us songs he learned at the Y camp, "John Jacob Jingleheimer Schmidt" and "My name is Yon Yonson, I come from Visconsin."

Those days were very special because of the closeness we shared. I remember how well Ed protected us. For my ninth birthday, he gave me a treat: He let me hop fences with him and his buddies to, of all things, raid fruit trees.

Mostly we giggled and laughed, oblivious to the cares of the world. We had freedom as long as we were at the table at 6 every night for dinner.

PATRICIA EDWARDS · FULLERTON, CA

HOT SPOTS

Soup companies aim for the small fry.

1962 »

Slurpy Seconds

Where Campbell's used illustrated mascots, Lipton's showed real children in its ads and wasn't afraid to have them looking messy, such as this little girl with noodle bits stuck to her chin. The message, like Lipton's mix itself, is instant: Kids love it.

Mommy, can I have a bowl for breakfast, too?

Why not? Anytime, for that matter. New Lipton Chicken and Noodle Soup with Diced Chicken Meat is that delicious. Lipton plumps chunks of succulent white meat (white meat only!) and a shower of tiny fine egg noodles into a golden broth. Try it today. Better yet, try all 11 great soups from Lipton—the soups that taste like mother just cooked them.

TOMATO · BEEF NOODLE · MUSHROOM · TOMATO VEGETABLE · GREEN PEA · CHICKEN NOODLE · CHICKEN RICE · ONION · CREAM STYLE CHICKEN · COUNTRY STYLE POTATO

EAT SOUP AND KEEP WELL

Campbell's TOMATO SOUP

Your favorite the moment you taste it!

Taste the Tomato Soup that won for Campbell's a world-wide fame. Let your appetite revel in its racy, sparkling goodness. And you'll instantly realize that it is in a class all by itself. An exclusive recipe which only Campbell's can offer

you. A skill, an experience in good soupmaking which stand alone. Glistening soup-kitchens which are the marvel of the culinary world. No wonder Campbell's Tomato Soup has such a delicious and unequalled flavor!

21 kinds to choose from . . .

She's as healthy As can be And loves her Campbell's Just like me!

10 cents a can

LOOK FOR THE RED-AND-WHITE LABEL

Campbell's Tomato Soup

« 1933

It's a Kids Game

Campbell's adopted its Soup Kids, drawn by commercial illustrator Grace Drayton, in 1905. The mascots were so popular, they were made into a set of dolls. Use of the icons diminished in the '30s—note how small the girl appears here—but Campbell's brought them back in the mid-1950s.

Snowsuit Optional

Friends and forts make up for a lack of winter gear.

The suit I'm wearing today is crisp and professional. This morning, I chose a black-and-white blazer and skirt with complementary heels from the racks in my closet stuffed with clothes.

Sitting outside the courtroom, preparing to argue my client's case, I notice what others are wearing. Some outfits appear to have been just rescued from the hamper, sniffed and determined to be good enough for one more go. Others are sharp: tailored dresses and pressed suits and ties. I always watch the fashion parade—floral prints with stripes, ski jackets with miniskirts—and wonder what thought went into the ensembles. I also remember to say a prayer of thanks simply for having the choice of what to wear.

Winter came early when I was 11. More than a foot of snow blanketed the derelict autos and trash cans in our housing project in Pittsburgh, Pennsylvania, softening the harsh voices that called after children. One of my friends from across the street invited me outside to play. I had a sweater handed down from my brother, gloves and a jacket. What I didn't have were pants. I'd grown in the previous months and my mother, Anna Maude, did not have the means to buy me new jeans.

I opened a drawer in the dresser I shared with my four sisters, hoping to find something to put on. All I came up with were denim shorts, the kind that covered my thighs to my knees. Knee socks took care of the bottom half of my legs. I had to wear canvas tennis shoes or stay inside, as we didn't have the money for boots that year, either. I might have looked absurd, but I saw myself as a genius who had solved a problem.

My mother saw me leaving the house, paused, and looked away. What could she say? My friend made a remark about my outfit, but it was not unkind. We soon forgot all about it as we built a snow fort

and waited for boys to surprise with a barrage of snowballs. Someone else might have noticed that my knees were bright red and my feet were soaked, but fun won out over fashion that day. When we finished playing, I went home and soaked in a warm bath my mother ran for me. The water brought back feeling to my toes.

I earn a living now that allows me ample choice of what to wear. I buy what I need, even splurging sometimes on cute shoes. But my real joy is sorting through my closet and finding donations. I recall the pleasure I had wearing each item and hope it is just what a buyer at the charity shop needs.

But I swear that if and when I ever see a child playing in the snow wearing shorts, I'll find the nearest store and buy her a new outfit. Then I'll help her throw snowballs at the boys.

VIRGINIA AMIS · PUYALLUP, WA

Clothes were in short supply for Virginia and her 10 siblings, but she didn't let that stop her from enjoying life.

SNOW MUCH FUN

WELL-ROUNDED COMPANION

This snowman in our backyard orchard in Rising City, Nebraska, had a special feature—a neck sturdy enough for 5-year-old me to hug. Siblings Melanie and Jon helped build it, but our father, Jack, did the heavy lifting. Mom Hilvie took the 1962 photo after a fresh snowfall hid all the rolling tracks.

DULCIE SHOENER
WHITEFISH BAY, WI

BUNDLED UP

Kevin and I posed for our dad, Arthur Krueger, with our little brother Keith in front of a giant snowbank in 1959 in West Allis.

KATHRYN RIDDER • CHILTON, WI

MITTEN WEATHER

Firemen made a rink at the park in Maplewood, in the late '60s, where my daughter Mary Ann (in back), son Richie (center) and their friend Bucky and his cousins Frankie and Alice tried out their new skates.

MARY LOU DECICCO
POINT PLEASANT BOROUGH, NJ

Finding Her Place

Years later, she finally fulfills her true potential.

Retired from a successful 25-year career at the telephone company, I finally had the courage to try college at last.

Decades earlier, my older brother had warned me about the "old biddy" in second grade. Stout and grim with steel-gray curls, Miss Spencer was as different from Mrs. Raymaker, my beloved first grade teacher, as could be. However, I didn't find her all that bad. I put stickers on wall charts to mark my efforts and showed my flashcards to the class. Most of all, I liked my seat in the first row.

Miss Spencer's desk was at the back of the neat rows of desks, where she could spring up to loom over anyone who misbehaved, gave an incorrect answer, or put a head down on a desk.

The rows were a ranking system. The first was for the smartest kids, and the intelligence of each succeeding row decreased. The last row was for those for whom there was little hope. I felt sorry for the pupils who weren't first-row material, but, typical of the privileged, I never questioned the moral rightness of the system.

But first-row status came with constant risks. More than once, Shirley Mooney cried when Miss Spencer threatened to demote her. Joe, a lovable clown and one of the few boys I liked, wailed and begged when he was sent back. I determined that would never happen to me.

But one day, I forgot to bring back my weekly reader from home. Miss Spencer called me to her desk and tied a string to my middle finger. It was hideous—6 feet long at least—and I had to wear it for the rest of the day. Then she told me to move to the third row. Without a word or a tear, I made the change. With that, I sank from a first-row up-and-comer to a nonentity.

At recess, I rolled the string into a tight ball in my palm to hide my shame. I was grateful that Miss Spencer had at least removed the tell-tale twine before I went home. I never told my family, and certainly not my brother. Dispirited, I lost the joy of going to school.

It pains me now how fully I accepted that one teacher's judgment. I became a middling student, rarely asking teachers for help, and graduated high school with a C-plus average.

Years of achievement in my career followed, before I applied to college at 54. I graduated four years later from the University of Puget Sound with a degree in English literature. My GPA of 3.8 was that of a first-rower.

GLENNA COOK · TACOMA, WA

Glenna liked her front-row seat in second grade. She's sixth from the right in the first row here.

Joan was 5 when the new librarian, Miss Federgren, bent the rules in 1943. Dorothea Federgren continued to work for the Chicago Public Library for 40 years.

OVERDUE LIBRARY CARD

ANGELS DON'T ALWAYS WEAR WINGS, as I discovered when I was 5 and had just learned to read.

Every day I had 20 precious minutes at the Rogers Park Public Library in Chicago to pore over the saga of Dick and Jane before my mother returned from grocery shopping on Clark Street. I loved the new children's librarian, Miss Federgren, who often suggested books I might like.

One day she asked why I never checked out anything. "You could take some books home and spend more time reading," she pointed out.

"I would like that," I answered, "but I don't have a library card."

The lady in charge of handing out library cards had already told me that I had to be able to write my name in order to get a card. How I hated to admit that I could only print my letters.

Miss Federgren loved books and wanted her young patrons to love them, too. She certainly didn't want them encountering unnecessary barriers to reading. Now she was truly miffed. I thought I heard her sigh as she grasped my hand and swept us both down a book-lined aisle. "That is a situation that we are going to fix right now."

Adult voices murmured and rose behind a large desk as librarians conferred. Then, in a moment of magic, I was given a card to fill out. My childish printing almost covered the application, but I had the gateway to the world.

How Miss Federgren, the newbie, was able to cut through the red tape, I never found out. But shortly thereafter, the library's rule about writing was eliminated.

My library card angel gave me, and every child who entered that heavenly place, the gifts of knowledge, wonder and imagination.

JOAN WESTER ANDERSON
WHEELING, IL

WHERE DID SUMMER GO?

MODEL STUDENTS

The perfect kindergartner in Lakehurst, New Jersey, in 1955, I'm at the table on the left, with folded hands. My friend Barbara, legs crossed, is holding her artwork like a book.

KAREN CHARNEY VITELLI · TALKING ROCK, GA

—❝❞—

My sons Brian and Todd gave me a smile before getting on the bus to Owasco Elementary School in Auburn, New York, in 1993.

LEON JESSIE · AUBURN, NY

SEEING TRIPLE

We were the first triplets to attend Robinson G. Jones Elementary in Cleveland. In 1963, on our first day of kindergarten, the local newspaper ran this picture of us in ABC order: Allen, Bonnie and Colleen.

ALLEN WOHL · BEREA, OH

CALIFORNIA DREAMING

We all dressed well for school in 1953—that's me fifth from the left in the back row. I was 11, attending Colin P. Kelly Elementary School in Compton, California. The school was named for a famous WWII fighter pilot. It was a fun time—I'd like to go back for just a day.

TOM MANN · CENTENNIAL, CO

Fun While It Lasted

That was an act no one could follow.

 weeklong senior class trip by train to Washington, D.C., was a tradition at Cedarville High School in Ohio. There were 45 students in our class in 1960, and 27 of us went, including my good friend, Warren Hawk.

Among the group that traveled to the capital were several ornery boys who loved to play silly pranks. I hesitate to give all the details of our transgressions, but one experience happened

at the hotel, where I was with a roomful of boys, including Warren. As we became loud and rowdy, we thought it would be funny to lock one of our friends out of the room. When he began to bang on doors trying to find someone to let him in, hotel security showed up at our door. We got the message loud and clear that we would have to leave if we created any more disturbances.

We visited all the usual historical sites: the Smithsonian, the Washington Monument, the

David's classmate Kenny, in a prank of his own, appears twice in the panoramic shot. Warren is seventh from left; David is fifth from right.

White House and the U.S. Capitol, where we had a panoramic group picture taken.

Our classmate Kenny started out standing in the back row at the far left for the picture. As the camera panned slowly left to right, Kenny ducked and ran behind the students standing in the back row. In our class picture, above, he is standing at both the left and right ends of the picture.

Because of our escapades, we were the last class that was allowed to make the tour. After meeting

with the four adult chaperones who traveled with us, the principal ended the practice of having the senior class visit our nation's capital. For that, we had to apologize not just to the class of '61 but to all future classes.

Warren and I are still friends. This summer, my wife, Judy, and his wife, Ginny Ann, are planning their first visit to Washington, D.C.

DAVID HUGHES · CENTERVILLE, OH

We got the message loud and clear that we would have to leave if we created any more disturbances.

Trip Marks End of an Era

A small-town senior comes home with a new perspective.

Posing in Jackson Square in New Orleans, the seniors dressed in their best. Sherron is in the second row, second from right. Next to her in the row are trip chaperones Mrs. Smith and Miss Mitchell.

E each Midland School class chose where to go for its senior trip. Students held car washes and bake sales to pay for the trip. My mother helped me earn money by working on a farm dressing turkeys.

Seventeen small-town and country kids left Greene County, Indiana—some for the first time—in May 1963 to experience the world without parents. Mrs. Agnes Smith and Miss Bernice Mitchell, two brave teachers with hearts of gold and nerves of steel, accompanied us. The ladies drove their own Chevys, each car filled to the brim with students, to catch the Illinois Central from Evanston to Louisiana.

Crossing the salt marshes and Lake Pontchartrain as we reached Kenner was a thrill. It was the first time any of us had stayed in a hotel. Lush mimosa trees surrounded the Holiday Inn's cloverleaf-shaped pool, and its narrow stem led inside to the bar, which we stayed away from but observed curiously.

Pauline, Beverly and I roomed together. In the evening, Miss Mitchell and Mrs. Smith came to our room to warn us not to venture from the group because of the danger of being snatched and taken captive in underground trade. With only two of them in charge of 17 kids, our clever chaperones might have resorted to a little "fear insurance" to keep us all from doing something stupid.

We toured New Orleans' French Quarter and posed near the cathedral on Jackson Square. Dressed up in our finest suits and dresses, we country kids were quite a spiffy bunch. I also fondly recall going for late-evening espresso and doughnuts.

Next we traveled to Biloxi, Mississippi. From our motel there, we crossed a bridge over the highway to the Gulf of Mexico. I sat on the beach with my best friends; it was the first time I'd ever been to the ocean. In the evening we went to a nightclub for dinner and a show by teen idol Mark Dinning. He pointed out our class in the audience as he sang—what a night!

The air conditioning on the train home went out, so it was hot and muggy, adding to the misery of the long ride. But as we waited in the school parking lot for our parents, I felt a deep sadness. The people I'd spent my life with were about to part ways, just when we'd grown up.

I look back on the trip with a mixture of joy and a lump in my throat, picturing us as we bade farewell to childhood days and moved on to new things.

Graduation day in the gymnasium was hot. My hands shook as we stood together as a class one last time on the stage in the old high school.

SHERRON FIELDS · BEDFORD, IN

Linda's classmates saved her after a bad "trip" in the late '60s.

LEAN ON ME

ALONG WITH OTHER HIGH SCHOOL students and teachers, I was one of 40 passengers aboard a Greyhound bus headed to an annual student convention. Used to trips in a family camper, I looked forward to staying in luxury at a prominent hotel in Houston.

After the first day of meetings and competitions, my friends and I found a cheap restaurant nearby. We quickly ate our inexpensive meals, worried our teachers might miss us. But as we hurried back across a parking lot, I tripped, falling hard on my knee. Only with the help of my friends was I able to hobble to our room.

By the next morning, I needed an ambulance ride to the hospital. I went back to finish the conference with an ice pack on my throbbing knee. In one more act of kindness, the hotel paid the medical bills that my family could ill have afforded.

LINDA CHISM · PLANO, TX

When Eric and David wanted to see change, they took matters into their own hands.

And the Children Shall Lead

Adults follow students' caring example.

The kindergarten class that entered Stanley Hall School in Evansville, Indiana, in 1957 grew up completely integrated. The old building had seen its first blending of races a few years prior to our arrival, but for us segregation was unnatural. We played together as friends and spent the night at one another's houses. But as we grew up, we began to notice segregation outside of school.

When I was in seventh grade my best friend was Eric Johnson. He was handsome, intelligent, and a born leader. Siggy (his middle name was Sigmund) and I, both preacher's kids, decided we needed to do something about the disparity we saw. Siggy and I organized an integrated Boy Scout troop. We were determined to make this a genuinely integrated enterprise, with six Black boys and six white boys. Together we invited each candidate until we had the combination we were looking for.

We had trouble finding a scoutmaster for the den, and though substitutes filled the role for some months, our troop disbanded during our eighth grade year. For that short time together, though, we learned about one another as we camped out, earned our merit badges, and became young men.

Siggy and I continued our friendship into high school. Freshman year he ran for class president, with me as his campaign manager. The only Black candidate of five kids running, he won over half of the vote from a class of 500, almost all of whom were Caucasian. He went on to serve as president of the student council during our senior year.

Years later I wondered if our friendship and our efforts to bring people together had had an impact. When my father died in 2006, I inherited his many sermons. Two in particular from 1965 and '66 powerfully promoted integration to our all-white 800-member congregation. I asked my mother, "Where did Pops find the courage to challenge this congregation in the mid-'60s in southern Indiana?"

"Don't you know?" she responded. "He got that from seeing how race made no difference to you and your friends. He saw how integration was much more natural to you than segregation."

That brought tears to my eyes. We had made a difference to at least one person—my own dad—who was moved by watching our example.

DAVID POLAND · LANSDALE, PA

Room To Grow
Dad's boots are tough to fill but Jay Smith
had a few years to think about what it would take.

ALMA COATES · HEMET, CA

CHAPTER 2

ALL IN THE FAMILY

Fun stories and delightful photos capture
the joy of spending time with loved ones.

MAY · 55

Glamour Girl

My hair is up in curlers and I'm wearing my favorite dress for grandma Lydia Dickman's birthday in August 1962. Family friend Nell is on the left next to my mom, holding Kevin, then it's Grandma and the rest of the usual cast of characters: my brothers Eric, Craig and Mark. They're dressed like they'd been working on their latest project.

LISA KRALL · DEWEY, IL

James and Margaret corralled Danny, Tim, Sue, Frank, Peggy, Mary, Kathy, Mike, Jim and Pat for free shoes.

Posing for That Shoe Ad Was a Real Kick

Herding 12 pairs of feet into a straight line
is no walk in the park.

M y family had never taken a group picture. But when you're raising 10 children, it's not a top priority.

In 1956, my father, James Cowgill, managed a linen supply service where we lived in Columbus, Ohio. One day while talking to a new customer Dad happened to mention that he had 10 kids, the oldest in her 20s and the youngest a toddler. The customer, Mr. Weiss, who was about to open a new shoe store in town, was completely astounded. He saw an opportunity.

"If you bring them all down for a picture in front of my store that I can use in an ad," Mr. Weiss said,

"I'll give each of them a new pair of shoes!" Dad couldn't get home fast enough.

Getting everyone together was a challenge. Jim and I, the oldest two, were out of the house, and Jim was always hard to track down. He was young and good-looking and loved to party. In fact, he was usually out having a good time with his friend Bingo, who had a monkey named George—who partied right along with them!

Years earlier, Dad had bought a used vehicle from the local funeral home because it had three rows of seats. Even that wouldn't hold all of us, but I had my own car and could ferry a few to the store

on the day of our photo shoot. As luck would have it, when I went to get into my car that morning, it had a flat tire. So Dad packed the funeral car with our mom, Margaret, and the kids and swung by to pick me up, too.

When we got to the store, we met Mr. Weiss, the photographer and Jim, who was grumpy. We lined up and everything seemed to be going well. But then Tim punched Sue so she started crying, Frank turned so his back was to the camera, and Jim kept frowning. The poor photographer was pulling his hair out.

"ENOUGH!" Dad yelled. We ALL marched to that drummer. We shut up, lined up and got the job done.

The picture appeared on the back cover of an advertising brochure—it took an entire page to fit us all in. It was the only photo taken of the entire

group of us until we got together for our parents' 50th wedding anniversary.

We kids are all senior citizens now, ranging in age from 62 to 82, spread out around the country. When we manage to get together the room rocks with laughter. Both parents had a great sense of humor and I've always felt that was their legacy to us, the gift of laughter.

The younger ones don't remember much about the day we took our family picture. But I do—like Danny the youngest posing in just his socks because he had already outgrown his only pair of shoes. And Dad having to shout to get us all to settle down. My daughter-in-law Joanne had the photo laminated and displayed at my 80th birthday party. My friends really liked seeing it.

PATRICIA COOK · PALM SPRINGS, CA

Two doves representing the star-crossed lovers fly next to the tree in the popular Blue Willow china pattern.

Preserving Fragile Pieces of the Past

Her mother's Blue Willow china tells many stories.

———

While I was dismantling the home of my mother, Rhoda Moyer, after her death, her Blue Willow plates called to me. We ate off them at every meal, but I never knew where they came from.

These plates witnessed many everyday moments at her table, including my father's midnight bites before bed, and my mother's tears during meals alone in her 35 years of widowhood. Once, over these very plates, she and I talked about my sister Delia's pending fourth marriage.

"I pray each night for all of you and for all of her husbands," she told me.

Knowing my mother said her nightly prayers on her knees, I quipped, "For God's sake, we have to stop her or you will never get to bed."

"Oh, shush!" she said, and laughed.

Then there were the moments of irreversible transition. Most visits home, my mother welcomed me with a hug and a question, "Are you hungry?" My answer—"yes"—would precede our heading to the kitchen, where she would make a light lunch and we'd talk about my six hours on the road.

But on one visit when she was in her mid-80s, after the usual query about food, I started for the kitchen. This time, though, my mother sat at the

Rhoda Moyer's daughters have brooches made from her china, below. Pictured in 1984 are Patricia, sister Rhoda (RoRi), their mother, Rhoda, Delia and Virginia.

If you look at a plate, it is all there—
the doves, the pagoda, the garden and willow tree,
and a dungeon maze around the edge.

table waiting to be served. I swallowed. I put our turkey sandwiches and potato chips on the Blue Willow plates, and we talked about her health over our lunch.

Stella was my mother's dear friend, executor of her estate and her unofficial fifth daughter. She was there for my mother in ways her four birth daughters, scattered across the country, couldn't be. On one visit home, I discovered that Stella had a pristine collection of Blue Willow china in a cabinet in her entryway. Dinnerware that was so familiar suddenly seemed rare and special in this dignified display.

The Blue Willow pattern tells a tragic love story. There are many versions, but this is one I like: The beautiful Koong-Shee is promised in marriage by her father to an old merchant. "Until that day you will hide your face from everyone but me," her father tells her. Koong-Shee's only friends are the doves that fly about the pagoda and willow tree. Chang, her father's servant, befriends the birds, and through them, Chang and Koong-Shee fall in

love. Chang rescues Koong-Shee just before her marriage. But her father tracks them down and throws them into the dark underground passages of the pagoda. Koong-Shee and Chang die in each other's arms and are transformed into doves, kissing above the pagoda and its garden. If you look at a plate, it is all there—the doves, the pagoda, the garden and willow tree, and a dungeon maze around the edge.

I looked at the cracks in the plates of my mother's that I had so carefully preserved. I decided to have brooches made for each of us who know this pattern so well—for me, my sisters and Stella's daughter.

In a note to each, I said that I hoped this small piece of my mother and her best friend might bring a smile and remind them of the stories the plates hold—the one stamped into the pattern and the ones we were all present for without our ever knowing it.

VIRGINIA GIANNOTTA · PITTSBURGH, PA

I Might Need It Someday!

Mother's saving ways save the day.

———

Years before the world got serious about recycling, my mother had considered it a mortal sin to throw away anything that might one day prove useful. The attic of our Victorian house was jammed with three generations' worth of family discards. I loved admiring myself in Cousin Hazel's silvery green 1920s evening gown and Grandma Heck's 1910 horsehair buggy cape.

Even after my mother moved to a smaller house, she clung to her saving ways. When she learned a government agency was paying several hundred dollars a pop for ashtrays, she was indignant.

"There are dozens of ashtrays in the basement that candidates for something or other gave away at the county fair," she said. "I'd be happy to donate them to the country."

My sister Alberta tried not to laugh. She asked, "Why would you save all those ashtrays? You never even smoked."

"It's wrong to waste things," Mother said.

Alberta pulled open a drawer filled with empty paper towel tubes: "And these?"

"In case I ever have to mail a photograph," Mother replied.

I pointed out that I couldn't remember ever needing to mail a photograph.

"You girls sound just like your father," Mother said with a sniff. "He used to grumble because I saved those twister things, until he needed one for an emergency repair on the lawn mower.

"Think of the pollution," she went on, "and all the beautiful trees cut down to make those paper tubes you laugh at."

The next day I was at Penn State's engineering department, doing research on the west of England. I copied several maps and managed to get them home without damaging them. Then I realized I needed a way to safely store them.

I'm not too proud to admit when I'm wrong; I picked up the phone.

"Mother, about those cardboard tubes..."

MILLIE BAKER RAGOSTA · BELLEFONTE, PA

MOTHER'S DAY GIFTS

Items designed to pamper or accessorize.

1949 »

Brush Her Cares Away

Toothbrushes were bestsellers for Pro-Phy-Lac-Tic (aka Pro-Brush Co.), but the company based in Florence, Massachusetts, had been making all kinds of brushes since the 1880s—after perfecting a plastic compound used for the handles.

For Mother on her Day... MAY 8th

Jewelite
BY
PRO·PHY·LAC·TIC

Delight her on Mother's Day with this gift of gifts . . . a Jewelite Roll-Wave Brush by Pro-phy-lac-tic. Supreme example of the brushmaker's art, the Jewelite Roll-Wave is scientifically shaped to conform to the scalp . . . to provide a fuller measure of beautifying action with every healthful stroke.

Other Jewelite Brushes, Combs and complete Dresser Sets, priced from $2.00 to $27.00, are available in delicate shades of Ruby and Sapphire, and in diamond-clear Crystal . . . luxuriously packaged in transparent gift containers. Jewelite is made by the makers of the famous Pro-phy-lac-tic Tooth Brush. Look for the name Jewelite on the package.

PRO-PHY-LAC-TIC BRUSH COMPANY
Florence, Mass.

Jewelite is also available in Canada at slightly different prices.

MOTHER'S DAY, SUNDAY, MAY 8TH

Started in 1842

Remember the one who never forgets —MOTHER

Whitman's
CHOCOLATES
P.S. A WOMAN NEVER FORGETS THE MAN WHO REMEMBERS

« 1949

Sweets for the Sweet

Already more than 100 years old in 1949, Whitman's was a trendsetter. Its artistic Le Brun box, designed for Mother's Day in 1924, is a collectible today. The Sampler, an instant hit in 1915, remains the brand's most popular product.

Mother of the Year Award

Mom knows there's always next year to earn that badge.

The year was 1953, and I was a proud fourth grade Girl Scout. I was such a compulsive badge-earner that the sash of my uniform was heavy with awards for sewing, boating, skating and gardening.

For my efforts I earned a scholarship to attend two whole weeks at Camp Chickagami, about an hour away in upstate New York. I was thrilled—now I could earn my camping badge!

My mother, Marie Grant, a Scout leader, helped me get ready. She sewed nametags in my clothes, bought me a canteen and a sleeping bag, and promised to feed my rabbit and write every day. I couldn't wait to meet my bunkmates, swim and canoe in the lake, and eat in the mess hall.

Finally the day came when we campers, about 30 of us, boarded the bus in my town of Cranford, New Jersey, to Lake Kanawauke, New York.

By the third day of camp I was utterly homesick. I missed my rabbit, my sister, my father, and even my cousin with whom I fought constantly. All my bunkmates tried to cheer me up. The counselors teamed me with a happy camper. My mother wrote every day, but her letters only caused tears.

I was sure my mother would realize the depths of my despair and rescue me as I walked on the desolate road to the lake. Disappointment that she never did brought more sadness. I stopped eating, and finally, unbeknownst to me, the counselors called home. The next morning, Mom, a relatively new driver and a poor reader of maps, headed for the camp, despite my father's opinion that I should stick it out.

Over 60 years later, I remember my joy when I returned from a hike and saw Mom sitting on my bunk! Although I was embarrassed in front of my peers, she held me, wiped my tears and said, "Well, Girl Scout camp isn't for everybody."

MARY DEMPSEY · MACON, GA

A serious Girl Scout, Mary, far right, thought two weeks at Camp Chickagami would be another feather in her cap.

The Groom boys, Joe, Jeff and Greg, wrap up their day with a front-row seat to a summer thunderstorm in 1957.

Sitting on the Porch

Brothers pick a favorite spot to watch the world go by.

 e grew up in a suburban area on the southeast side of Columbus. Our parochial school was a half block from our house, so we walked to school every day, and back home for lunch. The school and church took up several blocks, and we spent many a day playing on the grounds as if they were ours.

The front porch was always a favorite place for my brothers and me to sit and keep an eye on the neighborhood. We loved being out there in the summer, with the smells of flowers blooming and fresh-cut grass.

Our dad, Joe, was a butcher at Central Market in downtown Columbus. He rode his bike to work most days when the weather permitted. We never knew what he would bring home from the shop: ducks, chickens and even an octopus, much to Mom's dismay. Once he brought a lamb that we kept as a pet. We treated Lambert like a dog, complete with getting him a leash.

Our mom, Patricia, stayed home with us kids—by 1966, five boys and a girl. Mom was the family photographer and always kept the camera loaded with film to catch a perfect moment. She took hundreds of pictures and slides of us.

One summer night we were watching a storm roll in, and Mom found us in our favorite spot on the front porch, fresh out of the tub and ready for bed. Jeff had his nightly bottle, and I was clutching my trusty friend who never left my grasp except for a good washing.

I'm thankful for Mom's foresight in marking these moments. At 90, she's still taking pictures.

GREG GROOM · COLUMBUS, OH

This Sears Hazelton, at left, looks much the same as the design in the 1911 catalog, when it sold for $828. The Hazelton was available until 1922.

Family Fixer-Upper

A makeover brings this house back from the dark side.

We had only one day to find a home in North Lake. The real estate agent somewhat abashedly pulled into the driveway of a neglected bungalow. My husband, Scott, looked dismayed when I said, "This is the one!"

Orange and black striped carpet was glued to the front porch, and a metal grate covered the front door. Inside, the house had dark paneling, painted woodwork, green carpeting and a dropped ceiling with faux beams, but all I saw was potential.

We were the third family to own the house, and paid approximately 100 times the original cost. The 1913 structure built on the Sears Hazelton model had remained basically unaltered in all this time, decorating aside.

Now the fun started! We planned a full five-year renovation, starting with an interim painting project to cover the olive green colonial-style wallboard in the kitchen.

Over the next few years we spent winter months scraping, painting, stripping and repairing inside the house. My dad, Bob, restored the drawers and doors of the built-in china cabinet, which originally was a catalog add-on for $17.

In the living room, dining room and bedrooms, my Grandma Rose and I pulled off paneling and wallpaper. Throughout the house, we refinished the hardwood floors, and Scott worked on making the scary electrical system safe. In the basement, which was cool and dry, we found a root cellar and a large cistern that was no longer being used.

Before and after photos show work done on the living and dining rooms. Carolyn and her friends and family removed the false ceilings and paneling, repaired plaster, and painted and glazed the walls.

Heeding advice to alternate indoor and outdoor projects, we reroofed the house and made plans for a garage. Andrea, our daughter, and her husband, Matt, both architecture grad students, assisted with the garage design and construction. Friends helped us to put up walls and trusses, and my grandma painted every board we installed. We also repaired and rescreened all the double-hung windows and replaced the weight ropes.

The little house was a sad sight when we bought it, but after all our hard work, we now have a gem. We call it the Pumpkin Shell of North Lake, after the nursery rhyme phrase that ends "...and there he kept her very well."

CAROLYN FRIEDEMANN · NORTH LAKE, WI

CHICAGO OPERATION

DO YOU KNOW MUCH ABOUT YOUR ancestors? Were they honorable, righteous, law-abiding folks? Undoubtedly, some were, but those who weren't are certainly more interesting.

My grandfather Carl August Neddermyer just might be my most interesting ancestor. He was born in 1894 and lived in Chicago, Illinois. His father, Charles, was born in Germany. His mother, Frederika Johanna Christina Kukuk, called Frieda, was born in Woodstock, Illinois, and later moved to Chicago. Carl had many aunts and uncles.

When Prohibition began in 1920, the work of distilling alcohol went underground. My Grandfather Carl was one of those who was part of the black market. My mother, Elsie, remembered helping her father by putting the caps on bottles.

Some bootleggers, like Al Capone, made it big. But Carl, described as a small-time, lovable hoodlum, did not. In a picture I once saw of him, he was blond and good-looking.

In 1930, Carl was at an illegal establishment when he was shot. My mother remembered getting to see him in the hospital. As the story went when it was told to me in 1951, he lived 10 days before he succumbed to his wounds. He was 36.

Carl's death left his wife, Helen, my grandma, a widow with a 12-year-old daughter (my mother) to raise by herself. Grandma Helen later remarried.

LOIS PRITZLAFF · WEST ALLIS, WI

Carl's wife, Helen, raised their daughter Elsie alone.

Virginia commissioned local artist Leland McClelland to paint a watercolor of the house.

The Pursuit of Happiness

Their Liberty Home is the result of hard work.

*Gail Heffner-Charles submitted this history her mom, Virginia Heffner,
wrote about the beloved house she and her husband, Phillip Heffner Jr.,
built together and lived in for the rest of their lives.*

After a long search, Phil and I bought land near Lithopolis, in Fairfield County, Ohio. Our dream had been for our three kids to go to college, and Lithopolis residents' high school graduates are eligible for college scholarships from the Wagnalls Memorial Foundation.

The farm on Cedar Hill Road measured almost 19 acres, with two big ditches running through the front of the property that we used to create a pond. The dike formed a driveway and an approach to the house. For months, we studied floor plans, and we finally settled on the Meadowbrook design

from Liberty Homes' catalog of ready-cut homes. We reversed the blueprint and added a two-car garage. The dining room would become our music room, and we thought the lovely stone fireplace would prove to be the background for many special photographs over the years.

We excavated and laid the foundation, with Phil and me helping to lay drain tile and shovel gravel around the walls. Phil and his dad, Earl, built a garage and shop near the house site to store the wood and flooring until the basement was finished.

The first materials arrived in a semitrailer truck in July 1957 and included kitchen cabinets, oak

Digging the basement for the house in 1957, at right; aerial view of the property on Cedar Hill Road, below; Gail with her parents, Virginia and Phil, lower right.

flooring, doors, windows and trim. The boards were pre-cut and marked. Phil told the carpenter and his assistants to put away their saws and not to cut anything!

During the building process, our children rode with me from our current house in Groveport to school. I taught music half days at the elementary school and then I brought Gwen, the youngest, out to the property. After school, the bus dropped off Gary and Gail at the building site. Phil also taught during the day, so we met back at the house site to work in the evenings.

Throughout that entire fall, my electric skillet worked overtime cooking supper while we worked. The kids would bunk down in cots, and then we'd put them into their own beds at the Groveport house around midnight after we finished working.

The day after Christmas, we loaded up a moving van at our old house. The movers had some trouble getting the chest freezer out of the basement, and then the van got stuck in the front lawn. A heavy-duty tow truck had to pull the van out, which was exciting to the kids—but we were getting more than a little discouraged.

But finally, we were there. We unpacked the big moving van at our new home, ready for the many family adventures—fishing, cookouts, horses, dogs and cats, growing and canning food, sleigh rides, ice skating, posing at the lovely stone fireplace, weddings and receptions—that we were about to begin there.

VIRGINIA HEFFNER · LITHOPOLIS, OH

Phil told the carpenter and his assistants to put away their saws and not to cut anything!

A Better Life Across the Sea

Crossing back 93 years later,
a grandson visits the family homeland.

My grandfather Amund Amundsen Anvik emigrated in 1908, taking the *Lusitania* from Stavanger, Norway, to New York's Ellis Island. He was a fisherman in Seattle briefly, then homesteaded a 360-acre farm in Montana. In 1909, his wife, Ingeborg Johnesdatter, and daughter, Kristine Gunhild, joined him.

Arthur John, my dad, was born in 1910. When he started first grade, he spoke only Norwegian. I had the pleasure of going to my grandparents' farm as I was growing up, enjoying their Norwegian foods and accents. They died too soon, and I never got to appreciate them as an adult, but I always dreamed of visiting Norway. Dad encouraged this interest, often reciting the Norwegian table prayer.

In 2001 I finally went. I met my second cousin, Lars Eike, who told me about my Anvik genealogy reaching to the 10th century. I learned that I was related to King Harald III Hardraade, and became quite full of myself.

On another trip to Norway, I bragged to a young clerk about my royal heritage. She said, "Everyone in Norway is related to King Harald. Probably every Norwegian in America is, too."

King Harald, who died in 1066, had three wives. The following generations span 1,000 years, which adds up to millions of people. I'm still a proud Norwegian, and now I tell the Anvik girls that they don't have to pretend to be princesses—they actually are!

ARDEAN A. ANVIK • SHELTON, WA

Mayflower Voyage to the New World

Her ancestor cast anchor in Plymouth.

—

Part of my maternal lineage began in England and some ancestors of my mother, Janet, settled in Dedham, Massachusetts, in the late 1600s. No one traced her father, Arthur Eldridge, and his side of the family along the female line, though, until online ancestry searches became available.

Using genealogy websites, my cousin Cheryl Craig found a young Henry Samson was baptized in 1604 at the church of St. Mary's in Henlow, Bedfordshire, England. At 16, he set sail on the *Mayflower* in 1620. Henry came on the 10-week voyage to the new colony with relatives, but it is unclear why his parents did not sail with him.

Through researching the Eldridge line, Cheryl found that Henry was our 10th-great-grandfather and resided in Duxbury, Plymouth Colony. Unable to sign his name in script, he left his mark on deeds and a will. His possessions included "arms, wearing clothes, and a library." These were divided and passed on, along with land, to his nine children.

Henry was not our only seafaring relative. My great-great-grandfather Daniel B. Eldridge, a captain who died at sea, was buried on the coast of South America.

It's a pity that no one in my mother's family knew of this early Pilgrim ancestor. Thanksgiving holds a different meaning now that I know about my relative Henry Samson, and I am grateful for my cousin's research on him.

CAROLYN JACKSON · GAITHERSBURG, MD

Seafaring runs in Carolyn's family. Capt. Daniel B. Eldridge is her great-great-grandfather and the sixth-great-grandson of Pilgrim Henry Samson.

COME TO THE TABLE

JUST LIKE GRANDMA USED TO MAKE

Around a picnic table at Kilgore City Park are my older brother Jimmy, mom Edith, Grandma (who made the best fried chicken), Grandpa and Uncle Lester Phillips. This was in '49 or '50, before I was born.
MARY DAVIE · SACHSE, TX

GARDEN PARTY

As often as we could, my family got together at Aunt Lila's in Cottage Grove. At this picnic on her spacious lawn in about 1974, I'm on the far left, surrounded by my nieces and nephews. My older brothers Lyle and Dale are the guys in the back with beards.
SALLY LEE
ST. MICHAEL, MN

EVERY MEAL IS A HAPPY MEAL

Wherever the dinner, the activities were the same: eating, laughing, teasing and playing games. At this 1969 party, it was me, fun-loving Grandma Emma, brothers Eric, Shawn and Kevin, and dad Dayo.
LISA KRALL · DEWEY, IL

MADE IN THE SHADE

My grandparents George, far left, and Melinda Rolland, far right, packed up their nine kids and joined extended family and friends for a church picnic in western Massachusetts in the '30s. Facing the camera is Aunt Verna Bontempo.
EDNA GREENE · LEEDS, MA

Paula used her bike throughout childhood and college and well into her adult years.

From Rookie to Roadmaster

A shaky new relationship finds footing in a special gift.

My mother, Mary, remarried around the same time as my ninth birthday. I had a small celebration with my grandparents that day. My grandma made a luscious cake and I got some nice presents, but not the one thing that I had been asking—no, begging—for.

That week, my stepfather, Dean Hand, moved us to another state for his job, and I sank into a sulk. I missed Grandma and Grandpa, who pretty much raised me. I didn't know anyone in our new home of Sterling, Colorado. And I hadn't gotten what I wanted for my birthday.

Our block had many kids around my age, mostly boys. And they all had what I craved—a bicycle. But my mother was overprotective. She thought bikes were too dangerous for girls. Luckily, all the boys were very generous about letting me take a ride, which only made me want my own more.

Bikes in the 1940s were all the same standard size. You lowered the handlebars or the seat to fit a smaller rider. I was tall for my age, so I didn't fall off too often. But my mother wasn't happy about the possibility of me wrecking another kid's bike.

Even though my stepfather and I often clashed that first year—my grandparents had spoiled me and he wasn't used to being a parent—he took my side on this issue. "Let the kids play," he told Mom.

With my 10th birthday approaching, I began my campaign for a bike once again. My mother kept saying no, telling me that money was scarce and bikes too dangerous.

What neither of us knew was that my stepfather had secretly bought one for me and hidden it at a neighbor's house.

The morning I turned 10, there was a lovely blue Roadmaster with shiny chrome fenders parked right outside our front door.

That proved to be my most memorable birthday. It also marked a turning point in my relationship with my stepdaddy. He trusted me to ride safely and showed me how to take care of my prized possession. Later, he admitted that when he was a boy on the cattle ranch, he never owned a bike and always longed for one.

I rode that bike for over 50 years.

PAULA McLEMORE CORNELISON · AVE MARIA, FL

The More the Merrier!

Our neighbors Mr. Wendler and Kathy joined me, David and Mike for
a toboggan run in Milwaukee around 1958.

KATHRYN RIDDER · CHILTON, WI

CHAPTER 3

TRUE LOVE

These heartwarming narratives of first romantic encounters and long-lasting love are sure to bring a smile to your face.

Happy Couple

My wife, the former Mary E. Nuckles, and I cut
the cake on our wedding day on Feb. 5, 1955.

ELLIS T. BRANNAM JR. · KEENE, TX

Those Were the Days

Good times for newlyweds in '60s England.

R ichard and I were newly married when his U.S. Air Force unit was stationed at the RAF Wethersfield base in Essex, England. It was 1967, during the Vietnam War, and I took my first flight ever—alone—from New York at 19. I remember the ride from Heathrow Airport with Richard and his Air Force friend; I couldn't believe I was really in London!

At Mushroom Farms, where we lived, the houses were close together with only concrete instead of grass between them. I was so happy that our house was on a corner lot in the very back and had a little bit of a lawn!

We had to get used to a lot of things. Very few of the residences had telephones, so we used one at a neighbor's house a block away. I didn't get behind the wheel for the three years we were there—at first we didn't have a car, and then I never learned to drive on the opposite side of the road. I rode the bus to nearby towns, and we would take the train to London.

Our Air Force friends were from all over the United States: California, Minnesota, Alabama, New York, Ohio, Boston. We were all in the same boat—we liked England, but we missed home. We had parties every weekend. The guys dressed in suits and ties and we gals wore our best dresses.

From left: Patricia with Bobbies
and Big Ben on the Thames;
London fashions in front of
No. 10 Downing St.; with baby
Duane, born in England.

We also were friends with Richard's Air Force sponsor, Phil, and his wife, Letty, who was from Holland. Another couple, Lucie and Jimmie, lived with their baby girl in Braintree, a few miles away. Our young son, Duane, and I stayed with Lucie when Richard and Jimmie went on a mission that was outside England.

The English weather was very unpredictable. I would hang the diapers outside to dry until the rain started, bring them back inside until it stopped raining, then go out to the clothesline again. The rain made the rolling hills so beautiful and green; every night after supper we'd take Duane for a little ride.

We lived just 40 miles north of London. The first time we went to the city, I spent $100 on a blond wig and a stunning emerald green outfit with brown knee-high boots.

Richard's tour of duty was supposed to last only two years, but the Air Force wanted him to stay another year, so we did. As we left England we rode the bus one last time through Finchingfield, a picturesque village a few miles from the base. Richard loved the peaceful countryside and wanted to stay. We had wonderful times in England, but I was ready to get home to show off Duane.

PATRICIA WEBER · CASA GRANDE, AZ

I'd Like Some of That

The newcomer acted as if he already lived there.

When my sister Bonnie came home from the Peace Corps in Tanzania in 1966, I was working in downtown Milwaukee, so we found an apartment together in Little Italy, surrounded by Italian-American families. It was an eye-opening and enchanting change from the suburban neighborhood I'd grown up in.

After six months, my sister rejoined the Peace Corps in Korea and I was moving out. I'd just had spaghetti and meatballs for lunch when I heard a rap on the door.

It was the landlady, with three fellows to see the apartment. She was supposed to give me 24 hours' notice before showing up. What was I supposed to do? Of course I let them in.

She led two guys to the living room but one followed me back into the kitchen. "What's for lunch?" he asked.

Despite his brazenness I told him there was leftover spaghetti. While I washed my dishes, he opened my refrigerator door and helped himself, finding a pan and heating the spaghetti. He also served himself some milk before he sat down at my table to eat and chat.

His name was Larry. As we talked, I noticed the Marine tattoo on his arm—he'd been in Vietnam.

Then he washed his dishes, thanked me and rejoined his buddies. But before they left, Larry invited me to a neighborhood fair. I said yes.

We ate, went on rides and talked. And talked. And talked. Drinking a six-pack of Pepsi, we got pretty buzzed, maybe the reason I was able to stay awake to keep talking. Or maybe it was because we had so much to say to each other.

We compared notes on our upbringings. From a different side of town, he had been raised Catholic. I was a Methodist. His family had two girls and a boy, the same as mine. And he probably didn't ever want to get married. I didn't care unless I met the right guy.

The next week I moved to a new place with roommates while Larry moved into my old apartment with his buddies. He started showing up to my apartment on Sunday nights with a bag of George Webb sliders, whether I was home or not. My roommates liked that.

Larry and I kept talking and became fast friends. We got engaged on Easter 1967 and married in August 1968. And we still do a lot of talking.

MARY NARKIS · FORT ATKINSON, WI

After she saw him heat up his lunch and wash his own dishes, Mary figured she knew enough about the friendly stranger to say yes to a date.

Classic Is Better Every Year

A Lincoln convertible takes a couple through milestones.

M y brother came home one day in 1952 with his friend Herm riding on the back of his motorcycle. Herm looked like a nice guy, and he called me the following day for a date.

Herm didn't really have much time for dating. He was in his 20s, like me, and he worked six days a week. He also attended college at night.

But he showed up for the date driving a beautiful shiny black 1940 Lincoln Continental with the top down. In his hand was a yellow rose. Wow, I was so impressed! We drove to High Point Park in New Jersey, where he took a photo of me sitting on the fender of the car.

The Lincoln continued to be an important part of our lives: The year after we met, Herm and I went for another ride, to another park, where he proposed with a gorgeous diamond engagement ring. We were married the next year and drove the car on our honeymoon to New York's Lake George and Niagara Falls.

Our family grew and, with our two children, we toured many states with the Classic Car Club of America. Our children love the memories of those family trips.

On our 25th and 50th anniversaries, Herm and I celebrated by touring New England in the Lincoln. For our 60th anniversary, we had a big celebration at the local country club. We decorated the Lincoln with white balloons, and Herm parked it in front of the club. Our local newspaper featured us as Sweethearts of the Week.

After many wonderful years of marriage, we are in good health. And so is the Lincoln, well housed in our garage. Over six decades, the car has been wonderful, but Herm has been even better.

NADINE ROGG · GOSHEN, CT

In his hand was a yellow rose. Wow, I was so impressed!

Marian agreed to date Bobby, left, but she wasn't taking a backseat to Fanny, below.

Beastly Romantic Triangle

That's not how they roll in Altoona.

M arian, an auburn-haired beauty from Altoona, Pennsylvania, was a single, 20-year-old career woman in 1946. Marian loved her job designing storefront window displays at a popular downtown department store, and she dreamed of a career decorating the famous windows at Macy's in New York City someday.

She sat with her friend Anna, sipping sodas and watching couples at the local roller rink one day. Anna's newlywed sister, Janet, and her husband skated past.

"Janet's husband is very handsome," Marian said.

"Well, guess what?" Anna said. "He has an identical twin. I heard he's seeing someone named Fanny, but if it isn't serious, would you like Janet to introduce you?"

"No. I've heard a lot of stories about those rowdy boys from Hicksville. I think he would be too wild for me."

Two weeks later, the two friends were back at the roller rink listening to Perry Como crooning over the loudspeaker. A familiar-looking fellow skated over and spun to a stop.

"Where's your wife?" Marian asked.

"I don't have a wife, but my brother does," he said. "I'm Bobby. Would you like to skate?" Marian hesitantly accepted his hand.

A few days later, that rowdy guy from Hicksville showed up at Marian's door. Her heart pounded: Was he the love 'em and leave 'em type she'd heard about? He sure was cute, soft-spoken and a gentleman, and he smelled of Old Spice. He offered to take her for a creamy whip ice cream in his DeSoto coupe.

"What about Fanny?" Marian asked.

"Fanny? She's with me. Come and meet her."

Marian stopped in her tracks. What sort of idiot brings his girlfriend on a date with another girl?

Bobby opened his car door, and out climbed a monkey with the biggest brown eyes Marian had ever seen. The monkey sat on Bobby's shoulder and put her arm around his neck.

How rowdy can a fellow with a pet monkey be? Marian's dream of becoming a Macy's window designer faded, and my parents' romance began.

SUSAN SPRANKLE WALLS · TYRONE, PA

Let Me Introduce...

What was your name again?

This love story begins during a 1970s winter in one of those midwestern towns outlined in cornfields. After graduating from Bowling Green State University, I was teaching sixth grade in Whitehouse, Ohio. My music major helped me get a second job as a choir director at the Methodist church there.

At a church supper, I noticed a handsome sailor. He wore the latest wire-rimmed glasses, a trendy contrast to his military haircut and fatigues. His name was Terry and he'd deployed twice to Vietnam. He told me he was stationed on the USS *Gridley* in San Diego and was home to visit family. Terry didn't stay long, but as he left, he looked back across the room at me. *GI Joe meets John Lennon*, I thought.

After choir practice that evening, Pat, his mother, approached, saying she hoped I'd go out with Terry, saying he really liked redheads. I gave a polite excuse because I was already dating someone.

Two days later, a Friday, Terry invited me on a double date with his sister and her fiance. Terry called the next morning, offering to shovel me out of some overnight snow, and spent the day driving me on my errands. I felt like I'd known him forever. He left only when friends—including my boyfriend—were scheduled to come over.

On Sunday Terry and I were on the way to a family event when I asked him to pull the car over. I was about to tell him I was going to break up with my boyfriend when he spoke up: "I think I'm going to marry you." Without thinking, I replied, "If you ask me, I'll say yes."

With a marriage proposal accepted—two days after our first date—I had to introduce Terry to my family. Introducing him to my cousins Fern and Bob Wilt, I forgot his name. Fortunately, Terry saw the humor in this, and everyone else assumed I was overwhelmed by the new engagement ring on my finger. I really don't know how my parents got any sleep after that.

We had a long-distance engagement for about six months, then a June wedding in Toledo, Ohio. We spent three years in San Diego with the Navy before moving with our daughter, Emily, first to the Midwest and later to Westford, where Terry was the Veterans Service officer and I taught at the public schools.

Now retired, Terry and I have a trip planned to San Diego so that we can visit our granddaughter who currently serves in the Navy there.

LYNNE STADER · WESTFORD, MA

In one whirlwind week, Terry and Lynne went from being strangers to engaged.

Bring Back That Loving Feeling

High school sweethearts don't let it slip away.

Above, Sherry and Gene in 1961 at the high school prom in Cairo, IL. Thirty years later, they're all smiles at their wedding, right.

Luckily I was pitching and could see across the street in Cairo, Illinois, one summer day in 1956, because the cutest girl I'd ever seen walked past. I couldn't take my eyes off her. The softball hit me in the shoulder because I forgot to look at the catcher. I found out her name was Sherry Britton; she was 11 and I was 12.

The next Saturday at the Gem Theatre's double feature I spotted Sherry out with her friends. I mustered the courage to sit right behind her, then I pulled her ponytail to make her turn around.

Sherry and I were together for the next eight years. I played basketball. She was a cheerleader and the homecoming queen her senior year. I graduated a year before her and got a scholarship to a small school in Tennessee. We talked about getting married someday, but her parents were worried "someday" would come too soon.

After high school, Sherry went to study in St. Louis, and the letters between us became fewer and fewer. I visited her there and took her to a movie. I knew the relationship was over because, for the first time at a drive-in, we watched the entire movie.

I gave her a ride back to her dorm, kissed her goodbye and after that we didn't see or talk to each other for 26 years. I heard she got married and moved to Texas.

I continued with college, and coached basketball at the high school and college levels. Later, I got married and started a family. After a few years of coaching, I changed occupations. My new career was successful, but my marriage wasn't and my wife and I divorced.

I avoided going to high school reunions because I got tired of being asked about Sherry. And I really didn't want to risk running into her and her husband.

Then in December 1989, I went shopping at a mall I'd never been to before, about 50 miles from

where I lived. Someone grabbed me, and I turned and saw Sherry, just as beautiful as ever. Ten years earlier, her family had been transferred there from Texas, but she was now divorced.

We started meeting just for lunch, but we knew this was a second chance. We didn't want to lose another opportunity, and now—27 years later—we are still celebrating our re-found true love.

GENE CRIPPEN · JACKSON, MO

I couldn't take my eyes off her,
and the softball hit me in the shoulder.

PUCKER UP

YOU MAY KISS THE BRIDE

This is my favorite kiss with Gingie, as we kicked off our life together in 1967. Our wedding day was 30 degrees below zero, but we were warm.

DONN WOOD
HOPKINS, MN

The purple and black paisley tux was for my nephew's wedding in the fall of '72. I'm kissing my future wife, Renée Ewing.

CHUCK KAUFMAN · SOUTH BEND, IN

TENDER MOMENT

This kiss Robert "Bud" Smith gave Dorytha is one of the most romantic I've ever seen. The picture was taken soon after my grandparents were married in 1935, and he carried the photo in a pocket watch until he died.

TAMARA SAILORS · WEST JORDAN, UT

PERSONAL TOUCH

Popular personal grooming products helped suitors be their best.

1949 »

Well-Groomed

Barbasol was the first shaving cream, developed by a former MIT professor named Frank Shields in 1919. In the 1950s Barbasol introduced aerosol cans with the iconic barbershop pole design.

« 1949

Sweet Scents

First sold in the United States in 1929, Evening in Paris soon became one of the most popular fragrances for women and was given to many a sweetheart as a special gift to win her heart.

A Husband by Any Other Name

Personalized mugs were a gentle reminder of what might have been.

Call it a case of the man not taken. In the 1970s, I was in my 20s and had a boyfriend named Howard.

Todd was a new hire at my office, assigned the workspace next to mine. We became friends, and after about a month he asked me out on a date. But being in a committed relationship, I had to respectfully decline.

It wasn't long after that the inevitable happened: Howard picked me up at work, and he and Todd had a chance to meet. Their encounter was cordial, and in the months that followed, Todd never pressured me to reconsider his offer.

But his disappointment was evident in a subtle yet funny way whenever Howard was around: Todd would greet him by the wrong name. Instead, he'd call him some other name that wasn't remotely close, except that it started with an H—Harvey, Henry, Harold.

Eventually, Howard and I decided to marry, and we invited several people from my office, including Todd, to our wedding. Todd's gift to us was a set of four personalized diner mugs, each of which bore a different name: Harvey, Herman, Harold and Hank.

For years, the sight of those mugs never failed to make me smile and to remember my former co-worker fondly—because they came from Todd, and not Tony, Tim, Thomas or Terrance.

SANDY STERT BENJAMIN · LOS ANGELES, CA

Happy together, Sandy and Howard can always remember Todd's cups of human kindness.

Emma and Terry were happy to forego the chit-chat; below, on a date in 1955.

Silence Makes the Heart Grow Fonder

He didn't pay much attention...at first.

Emma Petty was a quiet girl, and she usually had a book in her hand. She was pretty, but to be honest, when I went to her house one Saturday afternoon in the summer of 1954, I wasn't planning to ask her on a date.

I wanted to go to a baseball game with Paul, her brother. He wasn't home, so I asked Emma to go with me instead. I found out later from her sisters that she didn't intend to go out with me, either. When she disappeared in the house, supposedly to ask her mother's permission, she was looking for an excuse to politely decline. Her mother and sisters convinced her to go with me to the game and have fun.

Our car ride into town was a quiet one. We were both happy not to have to fill the ride with chatter. We didn't mind just sitting together.

That was our first date. There wasn't much to do in Mount Juliet, but soon we spent time together however we could. We attended church and more ballgames together, and we loved going to the malt shop. We rarely went to the movies—my job paid only 50 cents a day and the movies cost a quarter.

I quickly came to realize that this quiet woman who always had a cross-stitch or a new book in her hand was the one I wanted to marry. One day I sneaked her class ring on my finger so I could figure out the right size for an engagement ring.

Before I left for Air Force boot camp, I asked her to marry me. She said, "I have to finish school first." So we waited until she finished school. And then we waited a bit longer, because the Air Force trained me on a plane they decided to retire just as I was finishing up schooling on it.

Our Thanksgiving wedding was pushed back, but on Dec. 23, 1955, we married.

TERRY HAMBLIN · MOUNT JULIET, TN

TENNESSEE ROMANCE

MY DAD, DUARD WALKER, WAS ATTENDING
Milligan College in eastern Tennessee shortly after the U.S. entered World War II. The entire campus became part of the Navy V-12 program, and Dad joined the Navy and shipped off to the Pacific, serving on the *USS Newberry*. Duard saw action at Iwo Jima and Okinawa before returning to Tennessee after the war.

Back in school at Milligan he met Carolyn "Blondie" Roberts. Named homecoming king and queen, Duard and Carolyn were an obvious match: They were both very athletic and loved all sports. Duard lettered in five collegiate sports; Carolyn played basketball and tennis, and was an avid bowler.

After graduating, both Duard and Carolyn coached high school sports, and then in 1951, Duard became the athletic director at Milligan. For the next 50 years, Mom and Dad lived in the dorms at Milligan, where they raised five kids. Dad coached basketball, baseball, tennis and track, and Mom stayed active in sports, continuing to be an outstanding bowler, as well as teaching us kids to swim. All five of us attended Milligan, too.

Duard's players learned that his coaching went beyond athletics, and some of them had distinguished careers of their own: Sonny Smith, who coached at Auburn, and Del Harris, an NBA coach, are two of the best known.

While my father was doing everything in sports, my mother was always a very big supporter. She was the rock behind it all.

GARY WALKER · BLUFF CITY, TN

Homecoming couple at Milligan, Duard and Carolyn went on to raise five kids at the small college.

NO APOLOGY NEEDED
My mom, Kaye Duncan, and dad, Joe Natale, went to the University of Denver. In fall 1941, Kaye was in the bleachers at a football game. She bumped into Joe, sitting behind her, and when she turned to apologize, he gave her a big smile. Mom was very outgoing, and by the end of the game, my dad, who was shy, asked for her number.

In 1942, my dad joined the Navy and was set to go to the South Pacific on a destroyer. Before he left, he asked Mom to wait for him. They got engaged when he was on leave in March of 1945 and married in January 1946.
JULIE MANN · CENTENNIAL, CO

With a Little Help from His Friend

It wasn't love at first sight, at least not for her.

During our freshman year at Baylor University in Waco, Texas, Eddie, my roommate, wanted to introduce me to a girl. She went to his church in Houston, and he and I went once or twice that year, but she was never at church at the same time we were.

The next year, Eddie and I were still roommates, and he gave me the same spiel about this "dream girl," who was now also attending Baylor.

In mid-October 1952, Baylor held a pep rally for the homecoming game against rival Texas A&M. Eddie rode with me to the rally in my new green 1948 Buick convertible, a car that had upgraded my social activity.

A few minutes after we got there, Eddie rushed up to tell me "that girl" was at the rally, too. Finally, I got to meet Charlene Morton.

Charlene and her friend Jean went out for Cokes with Eddie and me, but the rest of her time was filled. Charlene's high school boyfriend was also in town for the homecoming weekend, but I was able to wrangle a short date with her after her boyfriend went home.

On Sunday, I ran into Charlene and her entire family at a cafeteria. I talked with them briefly, and her mother was impressed I was the son of a Baptist deacon and "not bad looking." Now I had my friend and the mother on my side.

Charlene broke up with her old boyfriend, and our romance picked up a little steam. I was sure that she was the girl for me, and I thought she felt the same. When I called from Dallas to schedule time to see her over the Christmas break, I found out her social calendar was already full. I only managed to squeeze in one short get-together.

It was clear what needed to be done when we returned to Waco after Christmas: I quickly bought a ring to get this woman out of circulation. That worked, and we were married the next November.

Sixty-five years later, we're still a team, tackling all the challenges that life brings.

GORDON GRAHAM · DALLAS, TX

Gordon learned that a casual commitment was not enough to keep Charlene's interest.

Bronx schools were the backdrop for Rose Marie and Ralph's budding friendship, left. Ralph and Rose Marie De Natale, married over 71 years, below.

Elementary Romance

Kids knew it was a good thing.

Wy mother, Rose Marie, describes her love story with my father, Ralph, this way: "We met in the first grade. He kissed me in the coatroom in the second grade. He asked me to marry him in the third grade."

They met at PS 83 in the Bronx. When Rose Marie transferred for three years to PS 108 a few blocks away, Ralph never lost touch (or hope).

Rose Marie sometimes saw Ralph walking out of his way to pass her house on his way home from school. Summers, Ralph sent her unsigned postcards from the farm where he worked in the Catskills. Rose Marie had little doubt as to the "guess who?"

Rose Marie and Ralph were reunited in the seventh grade. On the first day, they spotted each other sitting at opposite ends of a long row in the auditorium, and exchanged smiles. By 16, my parents were "keeping company" at Christopher Columbus High School. One afternoon, Ralph's older brother spotted Ralph in the school library.

Leonard rushed home to report that Ralph was somewhere besides the football field, a sure sign that he was in love and that it was time the parents should meet.

Ralph and Rose Marie began their courtship. She went to his football games with her Brownie camera in hand to catch him in action; in turn, to this day, Ralph brags about Rose Marie's high school accomplishments.

Rose Marie graduated in 1947 and their wedding was a year and a half later. Rose Marie was 19 and Ralph 20, and though they had been in love for 10 years, some questioned whether they were rushing into things. But a shared background of Italian traditions and their Catholic faith supported the marriage. Weekly Sunday plans included a large midafternoon meal that intertwined the families.

My parents are now 90 and 91 and have been married more than 71 years. My mother reminds us that marriage needs to be worked on each day.

REGINA DE NATALE · NANUET, NY

Social Climbers

At 100, I enjoy my memories of more active times with my
husband, Fred. We were newlyweds in 1944 when this
picture was taken at Donner Pass in California's Sierra Nevada.

ESTHER GOLD · CAMARILLO, CA

CHAPTER 4

....

RETRO FUN

Remember Sunday drives with the family,
playing dress-up with friends and,
of course, eating Spam?

Rustlers Beware

My dad, August, took this picture of me dressed as my favorite cowboy,
Hopalong Cassidy, in our backyard in Detroit in 1951.

THOMAS HIRTH · CLINTON TOWNSHIP, MI

Shandell with Pamela in the saddle at the Columbiana County Fair in 1978.

Rodeo Contests Were a Barrel of Fun

This horse and rider set a fast pace.

Clarkson, Ohio, where I grew up in the '70s, was the epitome of small-town USA. There was just one crossroad and one streetlight on the cement pad where every kid hung out. Everyone knew everything about everybody.

My grandfather bought my first pony for my fifth birthday. I remember the ride home like it was yesterday, sitting tall and proud like I owned the world, on Apache, a beautiful, full-blooded Hackney pony.

I was in sixth grade when I discovered 4-H. It was heaven for an awkward kid with few friends to find people who were as horse crazy as I. For several years, I showed Apache, competing in shows every weekend, but the main event was the yearly Columbiana County Fair in Lisbon. Kids from all over converged on a dirty, dusty plot of land laced with "gifts" from the livestock, straw, mud, and the best and greasiest fair food ever. There were friends to be made and competitions to enter, and baths were nonexistent.

Apache and I loved the halter conformation competitions, which was basically me leading him around the ring and showing off how gorgeous he was. I, however, also wanted to go fast and barrel race, so the last year I competed, I rode my dad's horse, Shandell.

She was a senior quarter horse, but she had no idea older ladies were supposed to be reserved, quiet and slow. She loved the speed competitions, too, and even though we never won a ribbon, we had a blast. I competed in one class in which riders showcased how well their horses followed leg and bridle cues. I had the great idea to let Shandell show how quick she was and how tightly she could turn. The next day, an announcement was made that, going forward, a rider would be disqualified for stunts like Shandell and I had pulled. I wonder if that's still a rule.

That was also the year when I learned boys were treated differently than girls. It was an unwritten rule that kids could stay in the barns with their horses, and I was so looking forward to it. But shortly before the fair started, the board decided that only boys were allowed to stay in the barns with their animals. I was outraged. With the full support of my parents, I chopped my long hair off and wore hoodies to disguise my appearance so I could room with my buddy. It was a successful ruse and 4-H taught me, however inadvertently, to stand up for things I believe in.

I am so thankful for the time I spent in 4-H. It taught me that not everyone who competes for a trophy will get one, and that shouldn't be the goal anyway. The goal should be to have fun, make friends and learn about yourself, which I did and continue to do to this day.

PAMELA FOSTER · LISBON, OH

Shandell was a senior quarter horse, but she had no idea older ladies were supposed to be reserved, quiet and slow.

A QUICK WRAP-UP

Bob joined a 4-H club in his small Ohio town.

MY FRIEND STEVE ROGALSKI AND I
grew up together in Beallsville, Ohio, in the '60s. We were in 4-H and in 1966 we chose as our project a demonstration of basic first-aid bandages. Somehow that work at the county level qualified us for a trip to the Ohio State Fair.

Going to the big city to present to a large audience was intimidating. When it was our turn on the stage, we were given microphones to use, which had not been part of our practice routine.

As I demonstrated how to properly apply a sling to my victim, Steve, the microphone cord became tangled and got caught in the bandage: In one quick move, Steve had been slinged and wired.

I was embarrassed and didn't know what to do, so I kept going. Looking back, I realize that was just another valuable life lesson I learned from 4-H: When things don't go as planned, find a way around it and keep going.

Steve and I live far apart now, but one of the countless memories we still laugh about is our miscue at the great Ohio State Fair.

ROBERT ABEL
LINTHICUM HEIGHTS, MD

OPEN AND SHUT CASE
My mom, Diane, and her friend Donna were in the Troy Good Homemakers 4-H Club. The friends teamed up to do a demonstration at the Monroe County 4-H and FFA Fair in Albia, Iowa, in 1958. They built a storage box out of plywood, and upholstered it with vinyl. The demonstration earned a blue ribbon, and they were selected to present the project at the Iowa State Fair, where they received a blue ribbon as well.
KENDRA SINCLAIR · ALBIA, IA

4-H campers at the Michigan State College campus. Harriett is at the far right. Inset: Harriett's Grade A ribbon for her dairy project in 1936. Below: The Pontiac *Daily Press* ran this picture of Harriett Beckman as a young teenager with a Jersey cow at the Oakland County Fair in 1936.

CREAM OF THE CROP

AUNT HARRIETT, AS I CALLED HER (she was my mother's cousin), was raised on a dairy farm in Ortonville, Michigan. Her father was head of the Dairy Farmers Association, and Harriett was very active with 4-H.

I have her scrapbook: The first entry is dated 1933. She started her own neighborhood club, the Oak Hill Sheep and Dairy Club, named for the family's farm on Oak Hill Road.

Later, she attended Michigan State College (now University) and became a home economics teacher.

SANDRA SKENE
FENTON, MI

BEST FRIENDS FOREVER

PALLING AROUND
High school graduates in Portland, Oregon, in 1956, we ladies still get together. From left: me, Anita Simone Rose, Mary Dehen Helfenstein, Janet Meyers Terpstra and Myrna Beer Deets.
DOLORES SHEA

BIKE BROS
Buddies since kindergarten, in 1946 we were the four musketeers of East Grand Forks, Minnesota. John Westrem, left, later went to college and Tom Meagher, Orville Hodge and I went into the military.
RICHARD DuFAULT
LA MIRADA, CA

COME ON IN, THE WATER'S FINE!
My very best friend, Shirley (McLagen) Cain, left, and I couldn't imagine anything in the world more fun than filling two laundry pails in my backyard in Toronto in 1946 or '47. We didn't have a worry in the world, and we felt like millionaires!
EVELYN NUGENT · RICHMOND, ON

BEST FRIENDS FOREVER

⌃ READY TO TAKE ON THE WORLD

After graduation in 1947, my mom, Ginny Lindloff, and her friends went to see Desi Arnaz and his orchestra at the Hotel Sherman in Chicago. Pictured are Sarah Dellinger, Margie Shroyer, Mom, Rose Manis and Patsy Manuel.

JANET L. MOORE · MERRITT ISLAND, FL

» FUR-EVER FRIENDS

Poochie the pup and big boy Bonzo sit up for Ted Kaminski and me in 1934 in Chicago.

JOHN DANISZEWSKI

THE SAME GANG

I was behind the camera for this picture of my eight friends in 1959. We were graduates of Liberty High School in Bethlehem the next year, and to this day remain best of friends. From left in the foreground are Mike Delvechio, Dickey Schuyler, Jack Gray, Ken Venanzi and Joe Donchez. On the couch are Bruce Sames, Don Villani and Ned Fink.

LOU STELLATO · BETHLEHEM, PA

LIFE'S A BEACH

My friends laughed when I asked to be dug out on our senior trip to Atlantic Beach, North Carolina, in 1961. From left are Sandra Rideoutt Harper, Kay Phillips Williams, Patricia Arant Minschew, Kirven Mills and Robert Brock.

JAMES KING · ST. PETERS, MO

Ford's wagons were popular with many midcentury families.

Along for the Ride

Who needs a map when every road leads to gold?

——

My parents frequently took the whole family on unplanned outings when I was a young girl in Sacramento. On Sundays—my dad's only day off—my mother packed a delicious lunch with plenty of snacks and dog cookies, and we piled into our 1955 Ford Ranch Wagon with our cocker spaniel Sassy. Even if the weather was warm we brought along our coats because we had no idea where we would end up.

There were plenty of directions to choose from when we headed out on these trips. Whatever way we ended up going away from Sacramento, we were guaranteed to find a historic site. Dad would start driving as my parents discussed what might be of interest ahead. The trusty camera was always close at hand.

But often we never did end up at the historic site or town we set out for. That's because Dad loved to turn, suddenly taking another road that looked interesting. With that, we would be off on a new adventure, off course from the plan my parents had just made. The direction really didn't matter—the fun of the adventure was the mystery of where we'd end up.

Usually we ventured toward the foothills or mountains that surrounded Sacramento Valley. There, we found little gold rush towns, old barns and other spots.

At home, we had stacks of photo albums on the living room bookshelf documenting every trip—long or short—we went on. Friends and relatives who visited were trapped on the sofa next to the bookshelf and treated to a look at the pictures from our most recent adventure. I didn't appreciate all those pictures crammed into the albums then, but now I treasure the memories on the faded pictures in the crumpled albums.

My husband and I continue the tradition of Sunday drives, and have had many years of making beautiful memories.

SUSAN PEARCE · REDDING, CA

The direction really didn't matter—the fun of the adventure was the mystery of where we'd end up.

As more people acquired cars, entertaining the family with a ramble to parts unknown became a popular habit. With cheap gas and time to explore, aimless—or erratic—motorists sometimes slowed traffic to an annoying crawl, giving rise to the epithet "Sunday driver." This is a colorized promo shot for the 1939 LaSalle.

SUNDAY DRIVERS

KING OF THE ROAD
Dad loved to drive his brand-new '57 Ford Fairlane 500 around Erie, Pennsylvania, where we lived at the time. On Sunday afternoons, we'd drive down the steep hill to the dock in the bay to watch the boats on Lake Erie.
NANCY SCHAAF • MURPHY, NC

⌃ DIRTY DOZEN
All 12 of us kids climbed up for this picnic picture in 1960. One Sunday, Mom fried chicken, then we hopped in the truck—no seat belts or seats!—and took off to the zoo in Madison, 100 miles away.
DOROTHY TRANEL • CUBA CITY, WI

» NAVEL GAZING
Dad and I dressed up in our finest clothing for a drive through the California orange groves in 1947.
TOM MANN • CENTENNIAL, CO

STICKY SITUATION

On his drives over county roads around Chamois, Missouri, in the '50s, my dad, Huel White, never planned to stop and visit anyone. The main attraction was the scenery and "to burn some cheap gas." Every car he owned got great gas mileage, but they always needed oil, so he brought along a container of oil, just in case.

The county roads were mainly dirt, gravel and blacktop. One time in the summer, he drove on a new road, ignoring the signs that said to stay off. We got stuck in the blacktop, and a farmer had to pull us out with his tractor. It was back to dirt roads after that.

GLENDA FERGUSON · PAOLI, IN

Take the Exit To Paradise

When motorists hit the first modern turnpike in 1940, small roadside inns were the norm for stays overnight. As the roadway system grew, families had more choices. Postcards highlighted life-on-the-road comforts—and invited guests to help advertise.

NEON HOSPITALITY

This Holiday Inn sign was in Michigan City, IN, but it could have been anywhere. The signs beckoned to families with the promise of the familiar.

FAR FROM HO-HUM

Mom-and-pop motels in Myrtle Beach, SC, touted Atlantic views in the '60s, the golden era of the Grand Strand.

ON TOP OF THE WORLD

When it opened in 1927, the El Cortez was the tallest building in San Diego, CA. The world's first outdoor glass elevator was added in the '50s, giving riders views of the Pacific Ocean.

ALL THE COMFORTS OF HOME

The latest midcentury amenities lured travelers to this motor hotel on the oceanfront in La Jolla, CA.

The Tel-Star Motel's astro-themed neon sign lights up the strip in Myrtle Beach, SC.

Roadside Surprise

A family's restful vacation is rudely interrupted.

F ather held open the rear door of our brand-spanking-new 1955 Chevrolet for my sister Rita and me.

"OK, kids. In you go!"

Our mother had already assumed her post in the front seat. Rita and I scrambled in, excited to be going on our first real family vacation. It was a torrid dog day of a long-ago August, and we were setting off from our Cranford, New Jersey, home into the beautiful Virginia countryside.

Those twin villains of summer—humidity and heat—vexed us as we drove. Air conditioning was rare in the 1950s, and we certainly didn't have it. So the whole trip we fussed with the windows.

Cranked too high, they wouldn't allow enough cooling breeze. Rolled all the way down, they left us gasping in the windy cabin and shouting over the noise. The silly little butterfly windows were no help at all. We never did win the battle.

Fashionably Boiling

Our clothing choices didn't make things any easier. We definitely rivaled TV's famous Cleaver family. Our own June and Ward, mother, Ruth, and father, Michael, were primly dressed in the standard vacation outfit of the era—Mother in starched blouse, skirt, stockings and dressy shoes; Father in his best slacks, button-down shirt and dress shoes.

Godfrey Was Right

We coasted along the Virginia byways. At Front Royal, we stopped to spend the night at a small motel. Mother was in her glory.

"We're in Arthur Godfrey country!" she said, referring to her favorite radio personality. She drank in the sight of the scenic Blue Ridge Mountains, which Godfrey talked about in glowing terms on his daily radio show.

After a tour of the famous caverns, we headed south on Skyline Drive. What a picture-postcard view of the Shenandoah Valley from the crest of the mountains! Turning east onto Route 250, the warm day ripened into a sweltering summer evening as we cruised toward Charlottesville. It was time for us to find another motel for the night.

Shoeshine Elves

With the oppressive weather settling on us like a blanket, we finished our dinner and were anxious for bed. It was already dark when Father found a small motel that was brightly lit and surrounded by what looked like quiet woods.

Most motels in those days were strictly mom-and-pop operations with their own unique amenities. This one had a feature that fascinated me—a large wooden box attached to the outside of each room door. At check-in the clerk told my father, "If you put your shoes in the box on the door, we'll shine them during the night and return them by morning. It's a complimentary service."

My father was delighted. "Nothing like a good shine," he said.

One Window

We were given a room on the second floor. By the standards of the day, it was really quite nice—simple, clean and large enough to fit two double beds. But with no air conditioning, the place was stifling. A tiny bathroom at the back had the only working window. Father opened it as wide as possible and left the bathroom door open for airflow. Then he put his shoes in that intriguing box and we all settled in for the night to sleep.

Unexpected Visitor

In the wee hours, our quiet slumber ended as we were jolted awake by the deafening roar of an oncoming train. Four sleeping bodies suddenly became jack-in-the-boxes. Pop! Pop! Pop! Pop!

Top: Motels like the Algiers in St. Petersburg, FL, were a part of the transformation of coastal towns into tourist areas. Bottom: In New York's Adirondack Mountains in the '60s, Melody Manor's sign in Lake George lists the amenities.

Clockwise from right: The Aloha Motel in Virginia Beach, VA; a room at the Gondolier Motel and the exterior of the Hialeah Night Garden Motel, both in New Jersey's Wildwoods.

We froze upright in our beds, terrified that we were about to be bowled over by a speeding locomotive. Our terror worsened when the train blasted its eardrum-piercing whistle. Suddenly— *BAM!*—the monster shot past the open bathroom window like a long, very loud missile.

When it was gone, Mother, Rita and I still could not move, but Father calmly got up and walked to the bathroom to peer into the darkness outside. Sure enough, there were the train tracks running just beyond the wall. Wide-eyed, he returned to the room. "If I'd stuck my hand out the window, I could've caught the mailbag!"

The Back Lot
Bone-chilling fright melted into peals of laughter. After that, we remained on our guard in case of a repeat performance, but no other trains came.

The morning brought freshly shined shoes and a clear view of the rear of the motel nestled against a railroad embankment. Father was just about right: He probably could have caught the mailbag, or lost an arm, had he stuck his hand out at an unfortunate moment.

Cherished Memory
Years later, my husband, Ed, and I bought a farm in the Charlottesville area. Of course, one of the first things I did was search for that motel. But modern-day Charlottesville looks nothing like it did in the mid-1950s.

Then one day I was driving along Emmet Street when the old place suddenly was in my view. The shoe shine boxes had disappeared, but the tracks remained. I chuckled to myself as I wondered how many other travelers over the decades had been blessed with an indelible memory of a train blaring through their motel slumber.

CAROL M. ELY · ROSELAND, VA

COOL COLLECTIBLES

Fun colors, ideal design never go out of style.

1965 »

Instant Classic

Crafted by American industrial designer Michael Lax, the Lytegem captured 10% of the market as soon as it hit shelves. Its pared-down profile of basic shapes—cube and sphere—with a telescopic arm makes for a textbook example of form following function.

« 1953

Neat as a Hairpin

Daystrom specialized in inexpensive dinettes for middle-class buyers, sourcing raw materials and making its own laminates to keep costs down. Today's collectors love the sleek features, especially the hairpin legs, which epitomize 1950s design.

10 for 59¢
Golden Sponge
Creamed Filled

Hostess TWINKIES CAKE

NET WT 13 OZS

PARTY PACK

Individually Wrapped

Hostess TWINKIES
Golden Sponge
Creamed Filled

The only thing better than a Twinkie is the value party pack!

Golden Oldie Still Fresh at 90

Nothing can replace the classic Twinkie.

From its humble origins as a budget snack cake, the delicious Twinkie achieved a status high enough that it warranted a spot in the Millennium Time Capsule. Twinkies briefly disappeared from shelves in 2012 when their maker, Hostess Brands, fired most of its workers and went out of business. Dismayed fans clamored for more Twinkies, and the new owner's relaunch of the beloved brand was a great success.

James Dewar, a savvy manager at the Continental Baking plant in River Forest, Illinois, in 1930, had a lot to do with the success of the confection. It owes its place as an enduring classic to the recipe that, at heart, is simple: a feather-light sponge cake filled with sweet cream.

Great Depression economics were the starting point for these cream-filled cakes, The Twinkie took shape when Dewar wanted to find a use for the bakery's shortcake pans, which were idle when strawberries were out of season.

Original versions were stuffed with a banana-flavored filling, but a lack of bananas in wartime forced the bakery to switch to vanilla cream in the center. Twinkies continued to sell like hotcakes.

After Hostess Brands declared bankruptcy in 2004 and again in 2012, it looked like the end of the line for Twinkies. New owners brought Hostess out of bankruptcy, embraced the brand's cultural status and regained market share.

The original recipe contained eggs, milk and butter, but today's treat has 39 ingredients, eight of them corn-based.

NATALIE WYSONG

A Meat for All Seasons

Built to last, Spam wouldn't quit.

American GIs ate so much of the stuff, they made it the target of their most withering mess-hall jokes: "Spam is a ham that didn't pass its physical." "Spam is a meatball without basic training." "Now I lay me down to sleep and pray the Lord the Spam don't keep."

But America's Allies in World War II credited Spam with saving their bacon. The Russians called it "Roosevelt sausage," and a grateful Nikita Khrushchev wrote, "Without Spam, we wouldn't have been able to feed our army." Britain's former Prime Minister Margaret Thatcher, who worked at her parents' grocery during the war, fondly recalled opening a can of Spam to share with friends on Boxing Day (the day after Christmas) in 1943.

Spam stuck around in Britain, where food rationing lasted until 1954. Its persistence in British culture may explain why it shows up in a hilariously chaotic sketch set in a cafe in an episode of *Monty Python's Flying Circus* in 1970. That sketch also is the reason we call junk email "spam." Early computer gamers in the '70s and '80s referred to repeated messaging as "spamming" because it reminded them of the repeated use of "Spam" in the Python diner bit.

Today, thanks in part to soldiers passing along their rations during the war, Spam is beloved in the former Pacific theater.

In Guam, residents annually consume an average of 16 cans per person, and in the Philippines, Spam is a staple. Hawaiians eat a total of 7 million cans of Spam a year, and Waikiki's annual Spam Jam every April is a signature food festival.

MARY-LIZ SHAW

Army Air Corpsmen in the Pacific during WWII named their camp Spamville after the tinned meat. Spam cans wore a budget label printed in just two colors during the war.

Bugs Bunny Is Still Cool at 80

An animation team turned the cartoon world on its ear.

An undistinguished character called Happy Rabbit debuted in Warner Bros.' cartoons in the late '30s. The small gray rabbit in "Porky's Hare Hunt" (1938) was a nonspeaking extra, with a manic laugh similar to that of Daffy Duck, one of that studio's stars.

In its effort to dethrone Disney, Warner Bros.' underdog animation team, working in a studio so cramped they called it Termite Terrace, was producing sharp, daring cartoons. On July 27, 1940, the studio released "A Wild Hare," which starred an unnamed gray rabbit with a noticeably edgier personality.

Casually crunching a carrot, the wisecracking rabbit baits a dimwitted hunter. Then, setting up the routine that would become old hat in the many cartoons that followed, the clever rabbit thwarts his hapless antagonist after taking him on an emotional roller coaster.

Tex Avery created that raffish persona in the 1940 film, which was nominated for an Oscar. Chuck Jones directed later animations, adding many of Bugs' sly cultural references and sendups of famous personalities. Other artists like Friz Freleng and Bob Clampett also left their mark on the character, who was consistently a magnet for trouble. Key to Bugs' style was Mel Blanc. The official voice of Bugs Bunny until Blanc's death in 1989, Blanc used a Brooklyn/Bronx accent that was as much a part of the rabbit as his long ears.

Fame never changed Bugs, even though he became the official mascot of Warner Bros., and an American icon in his own right.

NATALIE WYSONG

Bugs Bunny remains one of America's most popular cartoon characters.

Hasbro, which now owns Play-Doh, estimates that if you were to make a single ball out of all the Play-Doh ever made, it would weigh more than 700 million pounds.

Imagination in a Can

In 2020, Play-Doh celebrates
65 years of molding young minds.

More than 2 billion cans of Play-Doh have sold since it first hit the shelves at Woodward & Lothrop department store in Washington, D.C., in 1956. Toy company Hasbro estimates that if you were to put all that compound through a Fun Factory play set, you would extrude a snake that could wrap around the earth 300 times.

The world's most popular modeling clay began as a cleaning compound for soot-stained walls. The company hit the skids, hard, at least twice—in the 1920s and again in the 1940s—until an imaginative nursery school teacher convinced the compound maker, her brother-in-law, to think of his product in a whole new way.

And soon there was no stopping Play-Doh. Once it caught on in the late '50s and early '60s, demand was so high, Play-Doh was back-ordered for 16 months.

In the years since, all kinds of fun facts have accumulated about Play-Doh, but the oddest may be this: On the toy's 50th anniversary in 2005, Demeter Fragrance created Play-Doh perfume.

Then again, perhaps it isn't so odd, after all. Anyone who grew up handling the clay recalls its distinctive aroma, which Hasbro described in a 2017 trademark filing as "the combination of a sweet, slightly musky, vanilla-like fragrance, with slight overtones of cherry, and the natural smell of a salted, wheat-based dough."

Or, as some might prefer to call it, the sweet scent of childhood.

MARY-LIZ SHAW

Brilliance Can't Be Rushed

The ideal prank, like a fine wine, needs time to mature.

My hometown of Ossian threw a big party in celebration of its centennial in 1950. There were carnival rides set up on Main Street and various games of skill. One involved tipping milk bottles for prizes. I won a small sack of rubber maggots at this game. They were so well made that when they were placed on a flat surface, they would wiggle vigorously from even the smallest movement nearby.

I couldn't think what to do with the ugly things, but they looked so real, there was no question of their value. I stored them in a dresser drawer until some later inspiration led me back to them.

I came in from chopping weeds one day to find a home-cured ham cooling on a platter in the pantry. After cutting off a couple of slices for a snack, I realized that I might have discovered the perfect use for my fake maggots.

I sprinkled them liberally over the ham, and used a matchstick to auger holes in the meat and slip in a few little monsters with just their heads poking out. It was a work of art.

A couple of hours later, Dad came in from the field for a snack, and I joined him. Mom set the table and went to get the ham. She was a long time in the pantry, so I knew she must have spied my creation. Finally, in German, Mom asked Dad to come into the pantry. There was considerable whispering and then Mom said "See? They're alive." I couldn't see what was going on, but her comment suggested that she had moved the platter, making the little rubber devils skitter.

More whispering in German and then Mom declared, *"Ich denke nicht!"* ("I don't think so!") And out she came, carrying the platter at arm's length and heading for the chickens. I followed her and asked her why there was rice on the meat. Before she could answer, I scooped a handful of the "maggots" and popped them into my mouth.

Poor Mom. She nearly fainted. I held a straight face as I chewed for as long as I could, but finally broke into laughter. The game was up. I confessed before the delicious ham became chicken feed. Both parents frowned, unsure of their response, before they laughed, too.

Now and then, perfection is possible. It's all a matter of timing.

FLOYD GARDNER · ALTOONA, IA

It Walks!

A boy plays with a Slinky in this early promo shot. Engineer Richard James invented the Slinky by accident while doing war research in 1943, when some spring samples fell and "walked" off a shelf.

CHAPTER 5

AT WORK

From peddling ice cream bars to picking beans on the farm, jobs teach important life lessons and bring families together.

Working Hard...or Hardly Working?

My dad, Raymond, fed hundreds of workers as a Civilian Conservation Corps camp cook in Arkansas in 1933. He's on the left, with some boxing buddies. Boxing was popular at camp; Dad "managed" the most promising boxers by feeding them his best meals, and took bets on the fights.

ANITA GARNER · SACRAMENTO, CA

Newspaper girls take a break: Audrey, in front, on vacation with friends Dorothy and Jane, who also had paper routes.

Neither Cold Nor Wind Nor Gloom of Night

Stalwarts deliver newspapers in small mining town.

W e'd heard of newspaper delivery boys, but my sisters and I became newspaper delivery girls for the *Daily Globe*. Myrna, Marjorie and I were in the seventh, eighth and ninth grades in Wakefield, Michigan, a mining town near Lake Superior. The afternoon paper was published in Ironwood, about 15 miles away, We picked up our large bundle of papers from a nearby gas station.

It was March 1949 and we knew springtime's warmth would soon melt the gigantic snowbanks. But this evening was cold and stormy, and we could hear the wind howling in a way that made us long to stay indoors. As we divided the papers,

our parents urged us to dress warmly in wool coats, snow pants, and Grandma's knitted hats, scarves and mittens.

Darkness fell before we left home with our paper bundles. We trekked in a group until we reached a crossroads at the midpoint. There we separated and hiked alone to our various customers' homes. After we delivered all of our papers, we always met again in the shelter of a huge evergreen.

We had to lean into the gusting wind, and then we rushed to each customer's doorway. We'd put the paper behind the storm door or else hurry around to the back door, where we'd toss the paper inside. Sometimes we were entertained by

Audrey Johnson (below) and her sisters shared a paper route in the late '40s and early '50s. Myrna (bottom right) and Marjorie (top right) were close behind their sister in school.

the music from radios or record players that came from indoors.

Our customers' homes lined the road across from Sunday Lake Mine. Immigrants of many nationalities lived near the mine: Polish, Italian, English, Swedish and Finnish. Several of them said that our delivery of the *Daily Globe* was the highlight of their evening. One customer told us that he always felt restless if the newspaper was delayed in getting to his door.

On Friday evenings we would wait in our customers' doorways for their weekly payment. Sometimes they also handed us fresh-baked cookies or treats, or gave us a coin or two as tips. Some even offered us candy bars that we saved to eat at home while we warmed up after our work was complete.

My classmate Lois lived on the last section of my route. That March evening, I shrank from the spooky sounds the power lines made as the north wind shook them. The road had only one streetlight, and the wires wailed like ghosts on my long walk to her house. Lois' mom invited

me inside that night to warm up in the living room beside their wood-burning heater.

My sisters' customers had also offered time to warm up from the icy blasts of March weather, so the three of us arrived only a minute or two apart at our evergreen meeting point. Now we were eager to finish and get home to our mom's steaming cocoa and the warm fireplace.

As we got older, Myrna, Marjorie and I took different jobs, but we would always remember our customers' kindness.

AUDREY CARLI · IRON RIVER, MI

Pedaling for Pennies

Selling ice cream treats had some sweet moments.

W hen I was 14, I got a summer job selling frozen treats via bicycle cart in Madison, Wisconsin. I sold ice cream bars, Popsicles and Fudgsicles, all of which were stored in dry ice. Each treat cost 10 cents, and for each one that I sold, I got 2 cents. I had to sell a lot to make it worthwhile. All in all, I made about $5 every day.

I learned if I pedaled from the east side of Madison to the University of Wisconsin campus, I would sell out. It was a long way to go, and the bike was hard to pedal. Turning corners was especially hard because the bike would tip if I turned too sharply.

One day I was going along Johnson Street on Madison's isthmus, and I had to cross a big intersection with several railroad tracks. To my surprise, a passing train stopped right in the middle of the intersection, blocking the road. No cars could go in either direction.

The train engineer climbed out and made his way toward me. I didn't know what was going on until he told me he would like two ice cream bars.

Meanwhile, the drivers in the cars started yelling and honking at the engineer. He said, "You didn't think I would do that, did you?" Then he gave me a tip, got back in the train and got it moving again.

I was always very tired when I got home. At the end of each day, I handed my earnings over to my mom. We didn't have much money, and my job helped buy a lot of groceries for our family.

All in all, it was a good job, but I was glad when the summer was over.

ROBERT ROCCA · SUN PRAIRIE, WI

Ice cream and bikes are all part of summer. For Robert in 1962, it was a way to earn some money.

Learning
the ropes at
Wiemann's store
kept Jon busy
in high school.

Student of Retail

The after-school job was a good deal.

From 1955 to '57, I worked every day after school and all day Saturdays at Wiemann's dime store. My manager, Max Schulpius, was aware that child labor laws didn't allow me to work that much, but he also knew how very important the job was to me financially and personally, so he let me continue. From my perspective, it wasn't really work because I enjoyed it so much.

In Milwaukee, Wisconsin, Wiemann's was a local competitor to Woolworth. I started in the store's stockroom, moving stuff, breaking up the boxes and cleaning the store. When they hired a new stock boy, I shifted over to the sales floor, where I was the only male. Then Max started training me for a career in merchandising. He taught me how to lay out counters, trim windows, price items and deal with customers. He knew it all.

Max eventually moved to a different store that needed his expertise, and the founder's nephew, Hugh, got Max's old job. Hugh spent most of the day standing at the end of one of the aisles with a clipboard. I have no idea what was on that clipboard, but it couldn't have been very important because he hardly looked at it.

Most of my friends and 90% of my self-worth came from that great job. My high school yearbook included a few brief descriptions of the graduates' activities over the years. Some of my classmates had a list a mile long, and even the students who didn't care about school had at least been in Boys Club. My listing was simply "Jon Benz."

When I graduated, I moved on to a job that paid more. The move was a good one, since Wiemann's succumbed to Woolworth's size and power and, sadly, exists no more.

To the guys who were football heroes in high school, my job must have been pretty tame stuff, but I remember my days in retail very fondly.

JON BENZ · HIGHLANDS RANCH, CO

Life as a Bean Counter

Her summer job was taxing, but had a few quirks.

s in past years, in 1951 my dad, Albert Bolzenthal, had several acres of beans on my grandfather's farm. Early in the morning, we'd pile into the car for the drive to the farm in Shoto, Wisconsin, to pick the beans.

Dad worked a day job, so my mom, Sylvia, was in charge of making sure we cleaned the rows and didn't crush or pull out the bushy plants. Mom was a very fast picker; I was 12 and my brother, Francis, was 9, so the three of us did the serious picking. Often we got extra help from neighbor kids. My little sisters, JoAnn and Carole, came, too, but they were allowed to sit in the shade or visit Grandma.

In the late afternoon Dad came back to pay everyone who helped. We were competitive, and while we waited in line to have our bags weighed, there was a lot of guessing about who picked the most. Each type of bean earned a different rate. The big flat green beans were light and easy to pick, but paid the least. Wax beans had to be a particular shade of yellow, but they were worth a little more. Green beans were the hardest to pick, weighed the most and paid 3 cents a pound. After Dad took everyone home, he had to go back to pick up the beans and haul them to the canning company, where he was paid.

There were other bean growers in the county, and they needed a lot of pickers. Bigger operations had buses that picked up kids. If we committed to picking for them, we had to keep our word or it was likely the end of finding work in that field.

As an almost-teenager, I preferred going on the bean bus to picking for Dad, though it wasn't much different—a bigger field, more kids and a bean boss who wasn't Mom. There was still the outhouse, the communal water dipper and a competition at the end of the day. I always brought a bag lunch of peanut butter and jelly on white bread. (Oh, how I wanted Wonder Bread, but it was too expensive.) The growers looked out for us, reminding us to wear our straw hats, drink water and rest in the shade if we seemed to need it.

Picking beans was an important part of my growing up: I learned to be on time, to answer to a boss and that my pay would directly reflect my effort. Most days I made $3 to $4; one day I made just over $1 after I found a snake under a bush and moved very cautiously the rest of the day; and a few days I made $5 to $6. I learned to spend that money wisely, since I'd worked really hard for it. I also learned that it's OK to reward yourself. Dad always gave us some time off to go to the county fair, and we enjoyed every minute of spending our hard-earned money on rides, arcade games and cotton candy.

Bean picking season the following year turned out quite differently for our family. There was no county fair for us—we were quarantined at home and Dad was in the hospital, in an iron lung, with polio.

JANET HAWS · TWO RIVERS, WI

Filling a bean bag was a triumph for JoAnn, 8, and Carole, 5.

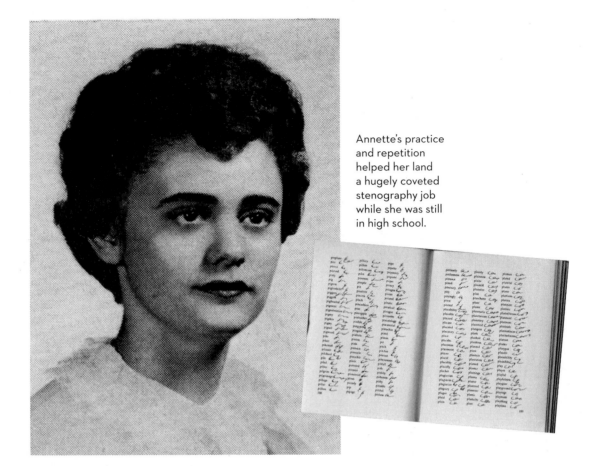

Annette's practice and repetition helped her land a hugely coveted stenography job while she was still in high school.

Shorthand Guide Long on History

Speed-writing proved a shortcut to vital life skills.

D uring my junior year of high school in Niles, Ohio, in 1956, I signed up for business classes; my friends and I envisioned ourselves as future private secretaries in prestigious offices.

Our shorthand teacher, Mr. Scobie, required his students to buy the miniature *Gregg Shorthand Dictionary*, which was only 3½ by 4½ inches but listed 28,774 shorthand forms.

In class, nimble fingers raced across steno pads as Mr. Scobie dictated at slowly increasing speed. Typewriters clicked fiercely as students transcribed their work into perfect business letters.

At home, I always studied my mini dictionary and challenged myself by playing hit records on our phonograph, jotting down those lyrics in shorthand, then transcribing them aloud.

My efforts paid off senior year when Mr. Scobie approached me with an amazing opportunity. He recommended me to Clare Westenfield, a local attorney who needed a part-time assistant.

Weak-kneed but with my trusty Gregg dictionary tucked in my purse for luck, I entered the Niles Professional Building through the revolving doors and took the elevator to the third floor. The kindly lawyer dictated a letter to me and, after reading the result, hired me to work part time after school and on Saturday mornings.

After high school, my love of reading and writing led me to become an elementary schoolteacher, but I used my shorthand in college. Later, I used it for lists or personal notes I didn't want others to read. Today, my failing eyesight makes reading that mini dictionary difficult, but even just having it near prompts thoughts of youthful years and promising times.

ANNETTE KOCHERA · BROOKFIELD, OH

Driven to Succeed

A son learns that hard work never hurt anyone.

Above: When Walter Allen Sr. started his delivery business in the early 1900s, a horse and wagon carried the groceries. Later, he drove trucks on his rounds for four grocers in Geneseo, IL. Facing page, clockwise from top: Mom, Dad and Walter Jr. worked at the gas station; Walter Sr. outfitted trucks for delivering groceries; Phyllis began driving a school bus in 1950 and stuck with it for more than 35 years.

For most of my childhood my dad and mom, Walter and Phyllis, worked very long hours. My dad held three, sometimes four, jobs to provide extra things for my sisters, Harriette and Priscilla, and me. My mother was a homemaker, but she worked several jobs outside the home.

Early in the mornings, I went with my dad to pick up laundry for Atwood Laundry in Geneseo, Illinois. At 7 a.m. he drove a school bus for George Pinks' Bus Service for the Geneseo School District. Dad talked Mom into driving a school bus, too. She was one of the first women to drive for Pinks'.

After dropping off the schoolkids, Dad delivered groceries for four stores in town. During the 1940s and '50s, grocery stores were typically privately owned, and they were much smaller than they are today. They were divided into three parts: Staples, canned goods and the meat department. Usually the entire store could be managed by only two or three workers.

Dad started in this delivery business in the early 1900s with a horse-drawn wagon. He replaced the wagon with a Model T truck, and later with a '36 Ford pickup modified for grocery delivery. When I went on deliveries with my dad, I could go into any of the stores and help myself to a snack of lunchmeat at the meat counter.

During the afternoons Dad was back driving the school bus, and in the evenings and on Sunday mornings he worked at Bollen and Smith's gas station, where my mom was a bookkeeper.

When I got older, I realized how much my dad worked, and I took a job at the gas station to help. Every night at around the same time, Vern Cobb would drive in for $1 of gas. Vern worked in the Quad Cities, about 23 miles away, so $1 worth (about 5 gallons) would get him there and back. I liked talking to Vern on his nightly visit since the job was boring when business was slow.

We lived in a fine though not luxurious house. We were always well fed, wore nice clothes and got a decent education. My dad also provided me with a bicycle, motorbike, motor scooter, pony and—on my 16th birthday—a car. We would not have had those things without both my parents working.

WALTER ALLEN JR. · ROCHESTER, MN

The Doctor Is in the House

In-person visits saved time and money.

Wearing a suit and fedora, carrying a black bag with a wide variety of instruments and medicines, my dad, Chester Widmeyer, was obviously a doctor. Doctors in the 1950s were given respect second only to ministers—depending on the minister.

Dad came from a family of tough West Virginia miners who moved to Akron, Ohio, to work in the tire factories after his father got black lung disease. One of 11 children, Dad was the only one to go to college, first becoming a pharmacist, then going to medical school at Ohio State University. He was the oldest student in his class.

Dad's office was above the pharmacy where he first dispensed medicines. He made hospital rounds early in the morning, then held office hours, followed by house calls my mother scheduled for him during the day from our home telephone. In the evening, we'd occasionally get a frantic phone call. I'd retrieve his bag from the side table, and we'd drive away in his Roadmaster. Dad believed that most of the time, the house call was effective for cases that weren't life-threatening, and it saved his patient—and him—a trip to the emergency room.

Typically I waited at the kitchen table while he treated the patient. Dad's deep voice reassured them, and he had family members help by bringing towels or applying gauze. Once I watched as he removed the longest splinter I'd ever seen, driven under a man's fingernail. Another time, I saw him straighten a dislocated shoulder—"simple, really," he told me on the drive home. One Christmas Eve, he delivered a baby. The young mother had hidden her pregnancy from her parents, and I'll never forget the sounds of the delivery. Dad came to the kitchen to tell me not to be frightened and he apologized for bringing me—though of course he hadn't known—and then he went back to his patient.

In his son's eyes, Dr. Widmeyer, here an Army captain in 1942, was certainly as big a hero as Cleveland's star athletes Jim Brown and Herb Score.

He charged $10 for a house call. Patients who lived outside Akron sometimes gave him bags of root vegetables or a cleaned chicken or two, or even traded carpentry at our home or his office. Dad was the least rich of his doctor friends, the only general practitioner of the lot.

Later, in the early '60s, he alienated these friends by supporting Jack Kennedy. Sadly for me, that ended poker nights—wild evenings of card playing and whiskey, the air foggy with cigarette smoke, and oh, the language! When Dad hosted, I would sit in pajamas at the top of our stairs, enthralled at the mayhem.

He died the final day of December 1965, when he was just 59. Months earlier, he'd seen the significance of the Medicare bill. "This is almost as important as penicillin," he said to me.

ROGER WIDMEYER · BRYAN, TX

After ninth grade confirmation in 1977, Scott stands with George and Marian at home.

Family and Fairness

Dad knew that working hard made life a little easier.

My dad, George, had an eighth grade education. A quiet man, he didn't understand my world of school activities. From age 14, he worked. And his dad, a stern German Lutheran, took his earnings and used them to pay family expenses.

I didn't really understand his world either: He was a livestock trucker, and I was certain I'd surpass anything he'd accomplished by the time I walked across the stage at high school graduation.

Summers in the mid-'70s were spent at home shooting baskets, hitting baseballs, or throwing footballs to prepare for my exciting destiny as a quarterback. In poor weather, I read about sports or practiced my trombone.

The summer before eighth grade, I was one of a group of boys a neighboring farmer hired to work in his field. He explained our basic task, fired up the tractor, and we were off, riding down the field looking for weeds to spray with chemicals. After a short way, the farmer stopped and pointed at a weed we missed. Then we began again. This happened over and over, but we soon learned to identify cockleburs, lamb's-quarters, foxtails and other grasses, and the king of weeds, the pretty purple thistle. It was tiring work, but I looked forward to the pay, even though I wasn't sure how much it would amount to.

At home, my dad said, "A job's a big step to growing up. I'm glad you will be contributing to the household." My dad's terse comment made me realize my earnings might not be mine to do with as I wished.

My labors lasted about two weeks, and the farmer said there might be more work, but I was not enthused. I decided it was not fair that I had to contribute my money.

When I brought my paycheck home—it was $119—my dad wanted to talk to me. Taking a seat at the table, he started: "When I was young I was expected to contribute to my family's support. I never thought that was fair. While I learned the value of hard work, I resented the idea that I owed my dad something as a kid being asked to do a man's job. Now, you saw the job through, and that's something to celebrate. Open a savings account, and if you have something you really want to buy for yourself, you have my permission. But spend it on something you can use and will value."

It was the longest speech Dad ever gave me. Only later did I realize how cathartic it must have been to do something for me that his dad had never done for him.

It changed my world, too. I had my eye on a yellow 10-speed, 26-inch AMF road bike, and now I could buy it. I had my dad to thank for teaching me fairness and hard work were always welcome in our house.

SCOTT BECKER · LAKEVILLE, MN

American Artistry

Jobs for millions of unemployed laborers were key to President Franklin D. Roosevelt's Works Progress Administration. It embraced artists, too. When critics balked, the WPA's Harry Hopkins shot back, "Hell, they've got to eat just like other people." Artists in writing, art, theater, music and history joined the WPA in 1935. Their work, a flowering of creative expression, continues to inspire.

MARY-LIZ SHAW

GRAPHIC DESIGNS
Posters in bold, saturated hues (below) were the signature look of the WPA. At left, Alice Selinkoff prepares a design for silk screening in the poster workshop of the Federal Art Project.

WRIT LARGE
Zora Neale Hurston, below left, Saul Bellow, below center, Ralph Ellison, Richard Wright and Conrad Aiken were among the thousands of wordsmiths employed by the Federal Writers Project beginning in 1935. Many worked on the American Guide Series—travel books for the states, territories and Washington, D.C., all highly collectible now. Hurston, an anthropologist, was among those who interviewed former slaves for an oral history of more than 2,300 narratives about life in bondage.

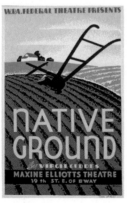

ON STAGE
The Federal Theatre Project led by Vassar's Hallie Flanagan, pictured at near left, put on plays for more than 30 million people over four years. One of the most popular was a 1936 staging of *Macbeth* in New York's Harlem, directed by a then unknown 20-year-old named Orson Welles.

LASTING VISION
Muralist Louise Brann works carefully on a four-panel fresco inspired by the European tapestry *Lady and the Unicorn* at the public library in Mount Vernon, NY, around 1936. Commissioned by the Federal Art Project, it still stands today.

IN LIVING COLOR
Seymour Fogel's *Security of the People* mural in the Wilbur J. Cohen Federal Building in Washington, D.C., is one of several created for the Federal Art Project. Under manager Holger Cahill, WPA programs commissioned 2,500 murals, 18,800 sculptures and more than 100,000 easel works between 1935 and 1943.

BUILT-IN BEAUTY
Even major WPA building projects like New York's La Guardia Airport, left, and the River Walk in San Antonio, TX, above, used artists to add flourishes, such as friezes and arches. The carved head, far left, by sculptor Albert George Rieker is one of four that decorate the war memorial in Jackson, MS.

Moving up in the World

In the pink in Greenhills.

My dear Dad had myriad jobs when I was young, including church sextant, production worker for Procter & Gamble, and janitor. Beginning in 1926, he served as a chauffeur and caretaker for the wealthy Harold Liddle family in Wyoming, Ohio.

Dad kept all the fireplaces lit at the "big house," stoked the furnace, cared for the grounds, serviced the cars and drove the limo—all for $30 a month and lodging. Six of us—my parents and we four kids—lived in a four-room cottage on the estate. It was the Depression, but we were considered poor even then.

When Dad heard about President Roosevelt's greenbelt community of Greenhills, he applied to live there. He got a job in the village's landscape department. So in 1942, we borrowed my cousin Otto's Model T truck, packed it with everything we owned and moved to an apartment on Chalmers Lane. It had two bedrooms, a kitchen, a living room, a utility room and a full bath. We thought we'd died and gone to heaven with that wonderful bathroom—indoor plumbing! And I swear the tough-built plaster walls were bulletproof.

In Wyoming, I'd been subject to prejudices because there was a caste system of rich and poor. But in Greenhills, everyone seemed to make the same amount of money. I think it drew people who had jobs and wanted to better themselves.

It was a very neat place to live, especially for teenagers. We could congregate at teen clubs and the drugstore.

THOMAS HAVERLAND · CINCINNATI, OH

Part of Thomas' story appears on newdealneighbors.com, an oral history of Greenhills by students at the University of Cincinnati and the Greenhills Historical Society.

AERIAL: LOC, LC-USF344-007483-ZB; YARD: LOC, LC-DIG-FSA-8A38399; POOL: LOC, LC-USF34-052002-D; POSTER: LOC, LC-USZC2-1093

COOPERATIVE LIFESTYLE

The greenbelt communities in President Roosevelt's New Deal were conceived by Rexford Tugwell, a trusted adviser to FDR and an economist who saw potential in urban planning to raise the quality of life for all.

Congress agreed to just three of Tugwell's towns: Greenbelt, Maryland; Greenhills, Ohio; and Greendale, Wisconsin. The towns were studies in utopian living, with tightly clustered housing, public areas and green space. Businesses ran as co-ops.

Greenbelt towns now struggle to keep their aesthetic identity amid pressures to redevelop. But all are registered as National Historic Landmarks, providing some protection for the future.

Opened in 1937, Greenbelt, MD, far left, was the first of the three New Deal greenbelt towns. All three communities featured amenities for residents and their children. The pool was a favorite in Greenhills. "You could get a family pass for about 10 bucks," Thomas Haverland says. "In the summertime, we lived at that pool."

Cold Calls

The family business kept customers on ice.

My father, Richard Mammoser, was the iceman in Hamburg, New York, from the late 1940s through the 1960s. The ice business was a family affair for our mom, Laura, and us five kids. Dad had several employees, his lifelong friends.

When I was 8 or 9, I went along with Dad on his regular deliveries. Customers placed an ice card in their windows indicating how much they wanted: They could order 25, 50 or 75 pounds of ice. Dad stopped the truck at each house and placed their order in an oak ice box, then collected payment.

Dad delivered to local taverns, where, on a hot day, he'd order a draft beer and I'd get an orange soda. They were a dime apiece. He also filled ice machines, and every Sunday around the kitchen table, our family counted quarters from those vending machines. We checked the date of each coin to determine whether it should be added to Dad's coin collection.

If the fire horn sounded during deliveries, the ice business came to a halt: Dad was also a volunteer fireman in Hamburg. Sometimes my mom had to fill in for Dad and drive the ice truck for the day.

In summer, there were additional deliveries. Every year Dad supplied concession ice for the Buffalo Raceway and the Erie County Fair, where the live fish tanks at the Conservation Building needed to be kept cool.

Dad's base of operation was the icehouse at Prospect and Hawkins avenues, where the ice was made. Tools of the trade were ice picks, holsters, shoulder pads and ice tongs. The temperature in the icehouse was between 15 and 20 degrees and even on the hottest days we wore heavy jackets, red wool shirts and gloves. In later years, the ice was made elsewhere and the building was used to store the ice before delivery.

The building is now used by the Hamburg Recreation Department; my great-grandchildren attend summer programs there. In one way or another, that building has been a part of our family for five generations.

DAVID MAMMOSER · HAMBURG, NY

The Mammosers delivered up to 75 pounds of ice door to door.

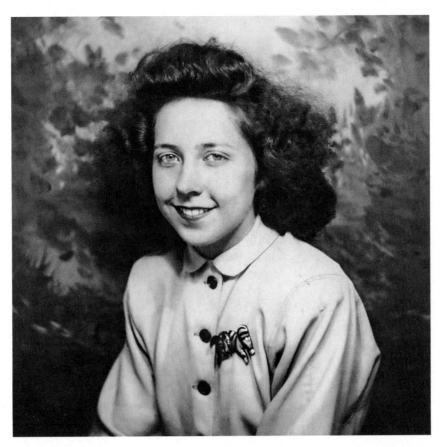

Tall Order for Young Waitress

This 14-year-old learned fast and kept her cool.

M y mom, Patty, was quite tall for her age, to the point where some movie theaters tried to charge her the adult price. But one time her height worked to her advantage.

The budget was tight for the Gayle family in the 1940s, so 14-year-old Patty applied for a part-time job at the coffee shop called the Purple Cow. She convinced the manager to let her work as a counter server. To his credit, he tried to verify that she was 16, but Patty "forgot" to bring her birth certificate until the manager finally stopped asking.

The coffee shop was at the Anderson Hotel, an exciting entertainment hub in Anderson, Indiana, and celebrities visited with some frequency. Patty remembered serving the famous "Johnny the Bellboy" Roventini, a well-known cigarette company spokesman.

She also waited on actor and musician Smiley Burnette. I remember him as Charley Pratt, the engineer of the Hooterville Cannonball on TV's *Petticoat Junction*. In my mom's time, Burnette was better known as Frog Millhouse, Gene Autry's comic sidekick. Smiley added "Frog" to his autograph for Patty, which he signed on a card promoting the restaurant's 65-cent special of beef stew, whipped potatoes and cabbage.

As an underage employee, Patty had one especially close call when her school principal stopped in for a sundae. Nervous, she took great pains to provide excellent service, including an extremely generous serving of ice cream. Patty's deception was never detected.

My mother graduated high school in 1947 and worked for 30 years in human resources for a local General Motors plant. But she never forgot her days meeting interesting people as a waitress at the Purple Cow.

LAWRENCE MILES · LAREDO, TX

Arthur Battisto, right, learns the art of the shoe repair business from his father, John, in 1939.

Father and Son Are Downtown Tradition

The shoe repair business was the right fit.

A rthur Battisto, 22, waited in line at the recruiting station in lower Manhattan to enlist in the Navy. It was January 1942, and ahead of him stood just about every young man in the city who felt it was his duty to join the war effort. Art didn't hesitate to do his part, but he held off on telling his parents, especially his mother, who cried upon hearing the news.

While Art was serving in WWII, his father, John, died, but when Art came home, he carried on John's trade of shoe repair. He opened Art's Shoe Service on Aug. 14, 1946, paying $25 per month for rent. Memories of the Depression were fresh, and shoe repair was a good business.

Art was my uncle, and just about everyone in Boonton, New Jersey, knew him as a beloved part of the town. He resided a short distance from his shop, and there wasn't a day in which he didn't go to work. In the early 1980s, a fire destroyed his store, but he worked furiously to rebuild it, never letting anything knock him down.

I loved spending time in Uncle Art's store. Everyone knew Art would go above and beyond to do an impeccable job. He shined all the repaired shoes to perfection, organizing the finished product for the customers to pick up. Of course, he loved to chew the fat (he liked that expression) with all the customers. His friends and some other business owners took a few minutes out of their busy days to relax and chat on the chairs he kept at the front of his shop. And when the annual Labor Day parade went past his store, my family and I got to sit in those front-row seats.

When I was young, I asked about becoming a shoemaker, but Uncle Art told me to work in another industry. He was dismayed that as sneakers and other styles became popular, people tossed out their old shoes and bought new ones rather than having them repaired. The business that got his family through the Great Depression was no longer worthwhile. When Uncle Art retired and sold his beloved store in 1996, it had become the oldest business in Boonton.

He always made time for people of all ages, and many regarded Art as a family member. I still walk past his former store and recall Uncle Art standing at the cash register, talking with all of his cherished customers or working diligently at the machines.

BARBARA BATTISTO · BOONTON, NJ

Forging Through

A man works in the glow of a smelting forge in 1942 in a Tennessee Valley
Authority plant near Muscle Shoals, AL. The TVA, formed to build up
the economy in the Southeast in 1933, still operates today.

CHAPTER 6

OUR HEROES

Stories of putting duty to one's country above all else, whether overseas or at home, move and inspire us all.

In-Flight Service

In September 1950, my mom, Virginia Caroline Wilcox-Spence, was a stewardess for Pan Am on a flight out of San Francisco taking servicemen to Asia as part of airlift operations in Korea. Pan Am commissioned several pictures of the servicemen posing with my mom, including this one.

JILL WORLEY · ANAHEIM, CA

Rude Awakening

The surprise attack shocks the nation and brings America into the war.

M y older brother, Austin, enlisted in the Army Air Corps right out of high school in 1939. After basic training, he was sent to Hickam Field in Hawaii, where he enjoyed tropical living— until the sleepy Sunday morning of Dec. 7, 1941, when Austin and his fellow airmen were awakened by what they thought was the usual artillery fire coming from nearby Fort Kamehameha.

But then they heard aircraft overhead. Austin looked out the window and saw Japanese planes dropping bombs and strafing U.S. aircraft parked in formation on the tarmac. All 10 of the base's B-17s were hit. Many planes were destroyed in that first wave.

Austin and a few others in his unit rushed to the supply hangar to outfit any intact fighter planes with tires so the craft could get in the air.

They were just rolling the wheels out when the second attack wave hit. A bomb dropped close to the front of the hangar, killing at least three men who were by the bay doors. Austin was farther back, which saved his life, but the monumental force of the blast threw him across the floor.

My brother suffered injuries to his feet, but he and the remaining men who'd survived the hangar hit quickly resumed their work.

When news of the attack on Pearl Harbor reached us, we feared the worst. We hadn't heard anything of Austin, and we had no way to contact him. Our mother, Catherine, said many prayers until, at last, we got a hurried three-word telegram sent along to us by the Red Cross: "Safe Love Austin."

In 1944, a friend and fellow parishioner in our church, John Diel, interviewed my brother about his experiences at Pearl Harbor. Austin told of visiting the Navy base two days after the attack. "It was a mangled mess," he said. He saw at least six vessels belly-up in the water.

Austin received a letter of commendation from his base commander for his actions under fire that day. He left Hickam six months after the awful attack and served in supply depots in the Pacific theater, including New Caledonia, the Solomon Islands and Guadalcanal.

"I'm pleased to note that even after all Austy has gone through," John Diehl wrote of my brother in 1944, "he remains his good, stolid, unspoiled self."

It was true of Austin then and stayed true until he died in 2003.

THOMAS HAVERLAND · CINCINNATI, OH

USS *Bunker Hill* burns after two kamikaze attacks on May 11, 1945, during the Battle of Okinawa. The attacks killed 372 and wounded another 264.

Threat from the Sky

A teenage mariner is witness to enemy's worst weapon.

A t just 17 years old, I was with the Merchant Marine in the summer of 1945, aboard the tanker SS *McKittrick Hills* and on my third trip overseas to a war zone. We were en route to the Philippines and Okinawa to deliver millions of gallons of much-needed fuel to Navy aircraft carriers. The invasion of Okinawa had started in April, and American forces were enduring heavy casualties. We were added to a Navy convoy, which gave us some protection.

Our first stop was Manila, once known as the Pearl of the Orient, but it wasn't a gem then. It was in ruins. While I was there, I contracted an infection in my right hand that caused it to swell and discolor. I was put on a Navy hospital ship, where a doctor who had tended to wounded men on invasion beaches throughout the Pacific theater treated me with a relatively new, powerful medicine called penicillin.

The greatest threat to sea forces at Okinawa were squads of Japanese suicide fliers—kamikaze—who came at vessels so quickly, they didn't always show up on our radar. Fighting those planes was intense. I saw a fellow crewman so distraught by the level of combat, he jumped overboard. Our ship alone had 20 mm antiaircraft guns that could fire 450 rounds per minute, but it was hard to be effective against high-speed aircraft once the pilot had a target in sight. And shooting down a plane didn't always mean we were safe. I recall one combat action where a kamikaze plane was shot up and portions of its fuselage slammed against our ship, damaging it.

MELVIN BOCKELMAN · LENEXA, KS

Melvin had a front-row seat to the Pacific theater as a merchant mariner.

The Will to Fight

He would have qualified for an exemption.
He volunteered anyway.

Raymond Widgren, left, flew 35 combat missions over Germany and earned the Distinguished Flying Cross while assigned to B-24s, like the one pictured.

My brother, Raymond Charles Widgren, was the second-oldest of five children and grew up on a farm in northwestern Michigan. While still in high school, he suffered the death of two brothers and his father—the last a few months before my birth in 1937. Raymond graduated a couple of years early and won a scholarship to Michigan State, but he had to turn it down so he could support the family. He took a job with the phone company, and a few months later we moved to the Detroit area.

In 1942, at the age of 21, Raymond volunteered for the Army Air Forces. As our family's main source of income, he didn't have to go to war, but he chose to serve. After doing his basic training at Harlingen, Texas, Raymond was assigned to B-24s in the 8th Air Force. He worked his way up the ranks to flight officer, serving mainly as a navigator. His base was in Scotland and all of his missions were into Germany.

Most men were lucky to make it through 20 missions. My brother flew 35. The day after his final mission, the plane and crew he'd served with were shot down, with everyone lost.

My brother didn't go into much detail about his experiences during the war. He did mention having served with James Stewart, the movie star who was an officer in the 8th Air Force. Raymond said that Stewart was a very caring and sincere man.

In July 1944, Raymond was part of an attack using hundreds of B-24s to disable some strategic German targets. During the mission, antiaircraft flak was so thick you could walk on it, he said. His plane lost two of its four engines and was shot full of holes, but he made it back to safety.

In October 1944, Raymond received the Distinguished Flying Cross for "extraordinary achievement while serving as navigator of a B-24 airplane on many bombardment missions over enemy occupied territory." He also earned three Bronze Stars with oak-leaf clusters.

Though my brother was never physically hurt, the mental wounds from his time in the war lasted his whole life. He was in his 70s before he talked at any length about his service. I was glad that after he spoke of it, he felt better.

RON WIDGREN · ST. LOUIS, MI

LAST TIME TOGETHER

WESLEY, HARVEY AND MARVIN BECKER, brothers of my husband, Walter, embrace at Thanksgiving 1941. All three were assigned to the USS *Arizona* at Pearl Harbor. At the time of the attack, Harvey was on leave ashore with his wife, Marie. His brothers had liberty, too, but they chose to stay aboard ship—Wesley, to save money, and Marvin, to pack for his trip home to Kansas for Christmas. His sole gift request: a jar of his mother, Freda's, pickles.

Harvey spent the first few days after Dec. 7 in a frantic search for Wesley and Marvin, but he knew in his heart that his brothers would have done their duty. Their stations were in No. 2 turret, where the 1,700-pound bomb that destroyed the *Arizona* hit. Official notice of their deaths reached the family months later. Freda kept Marvin's jar of pickles, still labeled with his name, in the cellar for many years.

CHARLOTTE BECKER · HAYS, KS

WORKING HARD AND MAKING DO

MY MOTHER, WILMA—OR "WILLIE," as her brothers called her—married my father, Art Sprester Jr., in 1941, when she was just 17. The war was raging, so their honeymoon was short-lived. Dad was drafted and was soon deployed to Asia.

Willie moved from Coleville to Bradford, Pennsylvania, to be closer to her mother. She got a job with Bradford Motor Works, which had been an oil field supplier but had transitioned to making fuses and adapters for bombs.

Mom spent 2½ years at the factory and worked rotating shifts, sleeping when she could, while also caring for an infant. She was proud when the company received an award of excellence for outstanding service to the troops.

Many food items and other everyday necessities were in very short supply because of rationing. People stood in line for staples such as coffee, vegetables, fruit, butter and sugar.

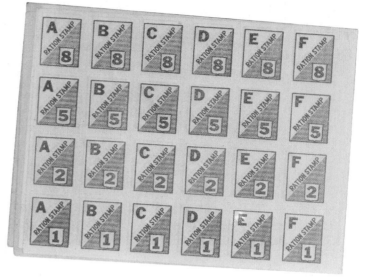

Young women missed nylon stockings, which were hard to come by. Either they painted their legs to look like they wore stockings with seams or "they just went bare-legged," Mom said. But everyone seemed willing to share these burdens of war.

At 95, Wilma has many memories of that time, but no regrets about the hardships. Everyone did what they had to do—that's just how life was then.

MARSHA BLAIR · MOUNT JEWETT, PA

Monthly rations of sugar and other goods were tracked in stamp books issued by the Office of Price Administration. These stamps from series three were issued in 1943.

PREPARING FOR TAKEOFF

My father, Price, built bombers at a Consolidated Aircraft Corp. plant in Fort Worth, Texas, during the 1940s. "This photo shows final assembly," he told me, and added, "I was in sheet metal to the left of where this was taken."
KEN GLASS · OLALLA, WA

PROMOTING THE WAR EFFORT

Businesses retooled, but the war didn't stop them from advertising.

1943 »

Optimism in a Bottle

The ad claims Coca-Cola is "the drink of our fighting men" and shows guys in uniform hanging out at a canteen, which would have been a familiar scene for many readers at the time. This follows a popular ad trend of WWII in which companies built trust in brands by showing they were popular with troops.

« 1943

Museum Piece

Illustrator Robert O. Reid takes a humorous approach to the serious subject of wartime rubber rationing. General Tire turns scarcity into a funny and positive message about the rare qualities of its tires. The ad also hints at the synthetics that later would dominate domestic tire production.

Two Soldiers, One Moment

Face to face, enemy fighters saw their
duty to the men behind them.

——

My father, Amos Flowers, told me the story of the two soldiers many times.
Shortly after his death, I wrote it down so it wouldn't be lost.

It was late December 1944, bitter cold, windy and snowy. We were somewhere along the German-Belgian border. I trudged through the snow, thinking of home. How deeply I yearned to be back on the farm in North Carolina with Mama, Dad, my wife, Grace, and the rest of the family for Christmas.

I was tired of the cold, the rain, the snow, the sloppy mud, the C rations and the stench of cordite and death. I was in Gen. Patton's 6th Armored Division, the Super 6th, in the 3rd Army, attached to the 106th Infantry. I'd never been away from home before being drafted. After going through basic training, I arrived at Camp Cooke in California and then on to the Mojave Desert to learn how to be a forward observer—a scout—an elite position for a naive Southern farm boy. And it came with serious responsibilities.

My job was to penetrate battle lines, determine the location of the enemy and radio that sensitive information back to our tanks. I was lectured constantly that the success of our mission and the lives of our soldiers rested on my ability to carry out my duties. I had a radio, a flashlight and a .45-caliber pistol. A rifleman was assigned to protect me, but more often than not, he was lost in the smoke of combat.

We crossed the Nied River in November without too much difficulty and without losing too many men, but it felt different now. Not since Normandy had the planning seemed so intense. A lot rested on our holding the line in the Ardennes forest.

As I clambered up a steep, rocky hill, I couldn't feel my feet. My thighs and back were rubbed raw from my uniform, which was saturated with wet snow and sweat. Slush dripped down the back of my neck from my helmet. I could see flashes and

Left: 84th Infantry troops advance through a field in France toward La Roche, Belgium, in January 1945.
Above: American soldiers crouch in a snowy thicket of trees during the Battle of the Bulge, circa 1944.

smoke on the other side of the hill. If I could just get to the ridge, I would know the enemy's location and could radio the tanks that were already on their way. My head down, I picked my way through the rocks. As I approached the crest, I looked up to see the silhouette of a German soldier against the flash of battle. He was only a few yards away and must have spotted me, too. He stopped abruptly. We stood there together, each unsure of the other's next move.

Then he turned his head slowly. I knew what he was looking for. He was a forward observer, just like me. I raised my flashlight to his face and the terror in his blue eyes told me that his rifleman, like mine, had disappeared. I weighed my options.

I was a good shot from years of hunting on the farm. But shooting him would give away my position and endanger the men depending on me. After a few seconds, he moved his head forward in a nod of acknowledgment, perhaps respect. I did the same. Then, hesitantly, we moved in opposite directions, each to his duty.

Later, we learned that we'd held the line and were instrumental in winning the war. That was not without a heavy price. There were 55 tank crews in my division. Only 11 survived. I was fortunate, but some of my friends were not as lucky. My cousin Joe Flowers didn't make it home. Nor did my best friend, Buddy Wells.

Now my responsibility is to make sure that those who didn't return are never forgotten.

SUZETTE FLOWERS CLEMMER · FORT MILL, SC

I looked up to see the silhouette of a
German soldier against the flash of battle.

J.C. Collins, here receiving a Silver Star for gallantry in action, tended troops through a freezing months-long march.

Medic Treated Fellow POWs

Doc Collins didn't turn down a chance
to get in the ring with enemy guard.

M y stepfather, J.C. "Doc" Collins, was a combat medic in the Army during World War II. He fought in North Africa and Italy, and after D-Day he landed in France.

Doc was captured Sept. 25, 1944, while tending his wounded troops. His company had pulled back, and it was raining. Doc wasn't paying attention to his surroundings, until a pair of boots appeared in front of him. When he saw they were black, he knew he was in the wrong place.

The Germans processed him as a POW, moving him to a camp outside Frankfurt, Germany. There, they allowed him to care for wounded and injured Allied troops, who were mostly pilots and air crew.

Doc was a Choctaw from Oklahoma and the Germans were quite intrigued with him. He used that to his advantage, managing to trade cigarettes with them for some wine. He saved the wine to give all the POWs a very happy Thanksgiving.

Doc had been a champion boxer back home. When the Germans saw him sparring, Doc got to box a Russian and a Frenchman, but his favorite was a camp guard. He told me, "I knocked them all on their coondog, but I really enjoyed smacking that German!"

In February 1945, the camp commander asked if the prisoners wanted to walk toward the American lines. All that could set out, but some had frozen or swollen feet. Doc stayed with them about a week, until they could walk, too. They trudged 345 miles to Lubeck, Germany, arriving in May. Doc spoke of the war but never gave details about that march.

Doc was soon on a boat to New York, very happy to be going back to Oklahoma. He was discharged, but then the Korean War broke out in '50 and of course he couldn't just stay home. But that's another story for another time.

WILLIAM H. BREWER · LEANDER, TX

Run to Freedom

After a daring mission, he was shot down and held prisoner.

About 20 miles outside of London, England, I was assigned to a B-24 with the 445th Bomb Group. On Feb. 24, 1944, we were in a group of 25 planes headed to Gotha, Germany. Our target was a factory that made Messerschmitt fighters. Unfortunately, we missed our rendezvous with the large wing of 200 planes that would have provided fighter protection. Nonetheless, our group leader opted to press on with his 25 planes, without protection.

Antiaircraft flak was heavy. When it let up, we saw a lot of enemy fighters. The Germans shot down 12 of our planes. Still, we found the target and dropped 2½ tons of bombs on the factory.

Ten minutes later, an enemy fighter attacked us head-on, hitting an oxygen tank, which caused our plane to catch fire and go down. Of the original 25 planes in the group, 13 were shot down, and nine of the surviving 12 had battle damage. Our group was credited with shooting down 21 enemy planes, including an ME-210 we hit before going down.

I survived the crash, but I was taken prisoner. I was held 421 days before I escaped on April 15, 1945. I was with the British Army—I even wore one of their uniforms—for five days before I was returned to the Americans.

I was at Lucky Strike camp in Le Havre, France, for two weeks before boarding a ship bound for home. I was close to the Statue of Liberty in New York Harbor when the war in Europe ended.

After the war was over, the U.S. government retrieved the bodies of four men from my bomber crew and buried them in a cemetery in France.

BOB TEICHGRAEBER
COLLINSVILLE, IL

Bob's Bomber crew didn't make it back after hitting a German target. He's second from right in the front.
Inset: After escaping a POW camp, Bob borrowed a British army uniform.

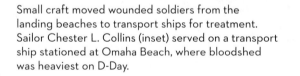

Small craft moved wounded soldiers from the landing beaches to transport ships for treatment. Sailor Chester L. Collins (inset) served on a transport ship stationed at Omaha Beach, where bloodshed was heaviest on D-Day.

ALL HANDS ON DECK

FROM 1942 TO 1945, I SERVED IN THE Navy onboard the USS *Dorothea Dix*. Part of Assault Force O-3 for the Normandy invasion, the *Dix* carried soldiers who were among the first to land at Omaha Beach at sections named Fox Green and Easy Red. As usual for these operations, there were reporters on the ships, and on this day, Ernest Hemingway was there to observe.

As we approached the beach, the English Channel turned rough, with waves 6 to 7 feet high, making many of the soldiers seasick. The ships offloaded the assault forces into smaller craft, and the troops left the relative safety of their group and proceeded to the beaches.

The *Dix* stayed on station, waiting for the return of the wounded from Omaha, which turned out to be the bloodiest site of all. As I walked across the mess deck, a doctor called me to help him dress a large wound on a man's back, even though 10 doctors and many medics were on board. When the ship was full of wounded, she headed back to southern England.

Whenever an anniversary of the event comes close, my memories become more vivid. My eyes have seen many things, but nothing compares to the sights of that day, June 6, 1944.

CHESTER L. COLLINS
CHILLICOTHE, OH

LATE-NIGHT KNOCK

MY FATHER WAS DOING HIS RESIDENCY IN SURGERY
in Rochester, New York, when I was born in 1940. In 1942, he was sent to serve with American forces in North Africa and Italy. I was devastated when he left.

On the night he came back home, my mother, Chloe; grandparents Julia and Horace Frierson; and we kids were in the living room when there was a knock at the door. Mother said what she usually did when someone called: "Chloe, go get the door."

I instantly recognized the soldier as my father. My younger twin siblings, Garth and Julia, ran upstairs in fright—the chickens—but I was delirious with happiness to have him back. I can feel it now as I write this.

Dad loved surprises, and he most certainly surprised us that night.

CHLOE FORT · SAVANNAH, GA

Joan and her dad had to get to know each other again after he returned home

CHANGES AT HOME

AT THE HEIGHT OF THE WAR
in 1943, when I was 12, my father, Clifford, was drafted. He was 37 then, and he had to leave his job in my grandfather's hardware store. Whenever I was missing my dad, I'd bike over to the store to breathe in the familiar scents. Dad served in the medical corps, so he was treating the wounded on both sides during the Battle of the Bulge.

During the war, our neighborhood in Philadelphia was called Post 10; our church sponsored a teen dance every Friday called the Canteen. My mother, Clara, taught us the fox trot, and we mastered the jitterbug.

We were visiting my aunt when Germany surrendered in May 1945. It was an incredibly joyous occasion when Dad came home that fall. But we didn't expect the changes to our routine. Mother then had to give up her two years of independence, and Dad didn't recognize me as the little girl he'd left behind. It took us time to get reacquainted.

JOAN PEACE · IVYLAND, PA

Chloe always remembers the delicious joy of seeing her father, Dr. Garth Edward Fort, return.

Sgt. Thomson was a platoon leader in 1968 when his plan to protect a young private took a tragic turn.

Out of Loss, a Lasting Bond

A friendship forged in war is cut short,
but love lives on for survivors.

M y dad, Mike Thomson, enlisted in the Army when he was 17, training with the 82nd and 101st Airborne and serving two years in Vietnam. He became a sergeant and fought in many battles. Dad told us about getting shot in April 1968, and being wounded by a grenade that June. But each year around Memorial Day, he became withdrawn and suffered from nightmares, and wouldn't say why. He told me once that it had to do with a man named Miller, who served with him in the war, but he didn't go into detail.

It wasn't until 50 years after Vietnam that Dad was ready to talk about Miller and the incident that haunted him. But my mom and I weren't the first people he told.

Dad searched for many years for Miller's family and finally located them in June 2017. He poured out his story to them in a long email.

Miller had also suffered a gunshot wound that April in 1968 and was assigned to my dad's platoon after recovery. Dad liked him right away. "He was a gentle and kind man who was a breath of fresh air."

The two became friends.

Dad's platoon was in Thua Thien province in South Vietnam on May 30 when the men were ordered into battle. Gunfire was heavy and the platoon was pinned down for hours waiting for help. The rest of the company finally reached them and carried out the wounded and dead. The platoon had walked in with 15 men and came out with four.

Knowing they would have to go back the next day, Dad wanted to protect Miller from another attack, so he had him moved to a platoon that was assigned elsewhere. But orders were changed at the last minute, and the two platoons ended up fighting alongside each other. Miller was killed that day by a rocket grenade.

Dad felt as if he had failed to protect the one thing he thought was good in Vietnam, and Memorial Day would never be the same for him. So he emailed the Miller family. They responded almost immediately. "My name is Judy M. Davis," the email read. "I am the younger sister of Pvt. Donald Robert Miller."

HONORING THE BRAVE
Floyd M. Satterfield, my brother-in-law, stands in the rain at a commendation ceremony with other Marines who survived the three-day Battle of Tarawa. Maj. Gen. Holland "Howlin' Mad" Smith was commander of the operation.
MICHAEL P. AUGUSTA · HONOLULU, HI

She went on to describe "our Donnie" as "a wonderful young man, a Sunday school teacher, a loving son and brother. He was an only son of an only son. His parents were Robert Miller, a World War II veteran ... and Florence Miller, the most wonderful woman in the world."

Judy kindly assured my father she didn't blame him at all for Donnie's death. "In fact, I want to thank you for trying to keep him safe. War is hell, isn't it? Least that is what my dad says when he tells his war stories. We grew up in a wonderful loving home."

It was an amazing moment for my father, who finally had the closure he needed. He'd carried the weight of guilt for so long without being able to speak about it. I was honored when he finally felt able to explain it all to me.

Three months later, my dad died of a heart attack while escaping Hurricane Irma. I was devastated and worked through the grief by poring over his war memorabilia. Eventually, I contacted the Miller family. They offered me the same love and kindness they'd shown Dad. My father left me a final gift in the form of the Millers' friendship. We are now close and contact each other almost daily.

Though I never met Donnie Miller, he has become a part of my life. Who would have thought that a tragic Vietnam encounter would bring two families together all these years later? I will forever remember him for my father's sake. And I know Donnie was waiting with a salute for my dad on the other side.

JODI KUCERA · YUMA, CO

It wasn't until 50 years after Vietnam that Dad would be ready to talk about the incident that haunted him.

BROTHERS IN ARMS

FORT DIX GANG

These five men and I were stationed at the Army's Fort Dix in New Jersey in 1961. From left are M. Jordon from Charlotte, North Carolina; Tom Willie from Peekskill, New York; William "Clancy" Maguire from Chicago, Illinois; and Frank Loeffler from Long Island, New York. The man on Clancy's shoulders is Robert Lavoie from New Hampshire.
L.K. BUTCH MILIUS · DENVER, IA

ONE NIGHT IN CAIRO
This picture of the men I served with in the Army was taken in Cairo, Egypt, in 1946. I don't have full names for all of them, but I remember everyone's last name. With me (left) are Bona, McCarthy, Siszinski and Ralph Brickman.
LOUIS ENGLE · CONSHOHOCKEN, PA

CHEERS TO THE SIX RAMBLERS
My father, Donald Yoe, and his Air Force buddies called themselves the six ramblers. Here, they were enjoying a drink at New York's Ringside Bar in April 1951 on their last night in the States before shipping out to Germany. Pictured: William Bowers, Bob Burns, Leon Stone, my father, Wade Arnette and Marvin LeDane.
SYLVIA METZLER
CHILLICOTHE, OH

Back at camp, John, right, and his pal Andy made sure 88 got food and attention.

Lucky 88

A soldier and his buddies brave danger to rescue a stray.

One of four brothers who served their country during the war, my father, John W. Wolinsky, recalls watching the Boston shoreline vanish as he left aboard the USS Wakefield on July 25, 1944, en route to Liverpool, England.

He was 23, leaving behind his bride of eight months. The thought of never seeing that shoreline again haunted him as the waterfront disappeared from sight. He was assigned to the Army's 551st Engineer Heavy Pontoon Battalion, where he earned the rank of line corporal.

His job was to assemble pontoon bridges, which were heavy-duty structures that supported the movement of massive tanks. During construction of the bridges, machines shot out clouds of white smoke to conceal the men from most enemy fire.

One cold September morning, while my dad's battalion constructed yet another viaduct over the Moselle River in France, the deadly German 88 set aim and fired steadily on the working area, which offered no cover. The company sergeant, in trying to stir morale, was hit and suffered the loss of both legs; many other soldiers were wounded or killed.

Amid the slaughter and deafening barrage, my dad saw a shivering brown and white dog. In spite of the horror unfolding around them, the soldiers of Company B rescued the terrified animal, taking him back to camp, where he became known as 88.

The men of Company B fed, watered, petted and played with 88. Caring for a dog served as a comforting reminder of life and boyhood, when the world felt safe.

When the war ended my dad returned home and mainstreamed back into civilian life. He took advantage of the GI Bill to attend carpentry school, which led to his involvement in the housing boom of the postwar years.

I'm grateful for my dad and others who came back and helped to make America into a safe place for their sons and daughters, and where dogs like 88 could be pets.

JoANN M. WOLINSKY · FORTY FORT, PA

Across the Pacific

My boyfriend in the 1940s, Porter Bowen, sent me this picture.
It must have been taken during the Pacific campaign in World War II.
He is the one without a hat, and his message on the back of the photo
made me laugh: "Save this for your grandchildren, Dot. Tell 'em you
went out with the best- looking guy in the world once."

DOROTHY HART LAMA • LINDSAY, CA

CHAPTER 7

....

MOTORING
MEMORIES

Favorite sets of wheels made everything
possible, from participation in after-school
sports to breaking down gender barriers.

Ready to Go

My first girlfriend and I looked prepared for adventure as we sat on the
running board of my family's Plymouth in 1936 Chicago. Oh, how
I wish I could remember her name!

PAUL ROSENE · ORLANDO, FL

Susan and Her Friends' Excellent Adventure

A cross-country trip in the '20s was a feat of derring-do.

My mother, Susan, lived a mostly average, uneventful life, never even learning to drive. But in the summer of 1929, when she was 24 years old, she embarked on an adventure. Susan Hess and four friends left Quarryville, Pennsylvania, in a 1926 Chevrolet sedan, bound for California. Two of the friends were Anne Geiger and Rena Rutter, but I don't know the names of the other two. All that is left of the trip is a photo album, with brief captions under each snapshot. The trip took the young women through a dozen states, and tracing the route on a modern map shows they must have

driven over 6,000 miles. Two or three weeks would have been required.

The travelers made at least three stops to visit friends and relatives en route. One was in western Pennsylvania, to see my mother's sister Frances. The women also made two stopovers in Indiana, visiting people whose names are unknown to me. For the rest of the trip, the women were on their own, spending nights in roadside cabins and at tourist homes.

Mother never spoke of discomfort, although with five people crammed into that little Chevy, nerves must have been frayed now and then. Tensions

Clockwise from left: Susan poses at Yellowstone; the car gets a wash; the Chevy is mud-spattered from dirt roads. Facing page: The little Chevy gets a repair.

probably were high when the group went through Kansas, where roads were deep with mud. It took a full day to get through that state, and while they avoided getting stuck, the ride was rough and slow. The entire car and their luggage and duffel bags, which were strapped to the front fenders and running boards, were covered with mud.

The photo album includes pictures of many spectacular sights along the way: oil wells in West Virginia, wheat fields in Kansas, mountains and lakes in Colorado, and Petrified Forest and Grand Canyon national parks in Arizona. In California, the group visited Yosemite, the Pacific Ocean, Lake Tahoe, an orange grove and a mission. The bold adventurers also saw a silver mine in Nevada, the Great Salt Lake in Utah, and Yellowstone and the Bighorn Mountains in Wyoming.

The performance of that '26 Chevy leaves people shaking their heads. Even loaded with five young ladies and all their gear, it seemed to make the trip without trouble. Mother spoke about flat tires (there were several), but she never told tales of breakdowns or even overheating. Certainly, the car must have needed oil changes and grease jobs, but she never mentioned anything like that. Of course, we don't have any information about the condition of the little Chevy after it finally returned home to Quarryville.

A few months after Mother returned from this trek, the stock market crashed and the Great Depression began. Had those young ladies delayed their trip until the following summer, it might never have been. I regret not asking my mother many more questions and taking copious notes. It occurred to me only later that her adventurous trip was amazing and unusual for the time.

WARREN ERB · LANCASTER, PA

Worth Another Look

An ugly duckling is transformed into a rare bird.

My Uncle Doug had a service station in Chico, California, back in the 1960s. A traveling salesman stopped to have his 1957 Packard Clipper Country Sedan fixed and never returned to pick it up. Doug was able to get a sheriff's title for it for $13. He eventually moved to Vale, Oregon, and over the years his family used the car as a daily driver. His kids learned to drive in it.

The car ended up in storage until 2001, when Doug decided to visit us in North Dakota. Before he left, he asked me if I'd like to buy the car, and without knowing anything about it or even what it looked like, I said yes.

When I first laid eyes on it I thought, What on earth will I do with such an ugly car? I considered chopping it up and customizing it, but my wife, Sheryl, objected when she learned that the car is very rare.

So except for the occasional joyride, the wagon sat in our barn for about 15 years. Finally, we began the painstaking process of dismantling it bolt by bolt, bagging and identifying each part. We tore it down to the bones, cutting out rusty panels and welding in handmade patches.

Factory replacements proved very hard to find, and I worried about getting it all back together. My father-in-law, Duane, knew a little something about the car's supercharged engine and helped rebuild the carburetor.

We've been to a few car shows since we finished the restoration, and we enjoy that it can mystify die-hard car buffs. A club dedicated to this long-lost brand gave our car the people's choice and best of show awards at a recent gathering. Yet even there, many people said they had never seen a vehicle like ours.

I'm so happy Sheryl and I decided to fix up this gem, which will be in our family for years to come. I even like it now!

CURT HUSSEY · WEST FARGO, ND

One Boy's Dream Coupe

Seen in a flash from a curb, it stayed with him.

W hen I was 11, in 1942, I lived in a quiet residential area of Los Angeles called Eagle Rock. I played baseball in the street with my friends, and when the occasional car came along, we'd move to the side to let it to go by.

I was impressed one day by a passing car that was long and sleek. It reminded me of the World War II fighter planes of the day.

But when I was 16, Ford was the vehicle to have. I bought a 1932 Ford coupe for $175. My next car, a much better one, was a 1932 Ford roadster.

In 1968, the company I worked for moved to the San Diego area, and for a while, airplanes held my interest. I got my pilot's license and bought a Piper Comanche with a friend.

Years later, after I had retired, my son, Bill, a painting contractor, was on a job when he spotted a dust-covered car in the garage. Bill negotiated a trade: the painting job for the car.

It proved to be the very model I'd seen and liked during the war, a 1941 Dodge Deluxe. With help from my other son, Rich, Bill and I restored it using parts from a junked model. It took all of us 10 years to complete the top-to-bottom restoration, but it turned out beautifully. It has factory accessories, including push-button radio, heater and clock. When new, the car sold for $825, plus $25 for the fluid drive feature, which allowed for fewer downshifts at stops or on moderate hills.

We've been driving it for a couple of years and have entered it in local car shows. I have owned 27 vehicles over the years, but I finally have the car I admired so much as a boy.

RICHARD KEMPLIN · POWAY, CA

Blast from the Past

A son's error in judgment reminds Dad of his own mistake.

My friends were driving Mustangs, MGs and even a Jaguar in 1966, and when I turned 16, I wanted a car of my own. I knew those cars were way out of my price range, but I mowed lawns and scrounged any odd jobs I could find to make money. At the end of a year my net worth was $150. At that rate, I was afraid I'd never own a car.

Still, I scoured the used-car ads in the newspaper. I finally found a 20-year-old Chrysler at an estate sale. The price was right on target at $150. My dad, Roy, warned me that a 1946 Chrysler would probably have half a million miles on it. I pleaded with him and finally Dad agreed to take me to see my dream car.

Well, guess what? The car was in mint condition, with just 30,000 miles on it. The owner was a druggist who walked the two blocks to his store every day and drove the car only to church and the grocery store. So after Dad OK'd the deal, I bought the car.

One day soon after, I was riding in a friend's car when he showed me a stunt. While going down a hill, he turned off the engine, pressed in the clutch and mashed the accelerator. When he let the clutch out and turned the ignition, the car blasted an explosive backfire. I couldn't wait to show this trick to my girlfriend, Linda Mackie.

"Watch this!" I said, and I repeated the steps my buddy showed me. But something went wrong: After the backfire the Chrysler sounded like a roaring dump truck. I pulled over to the curb, got out and looked under the vehicle. I didn't know a lot about cars in those days, but even I couldn't miss the gaping grapefruit-sized hole in the muffler.

At breakfast the next morning, I was nonchalant. "By the way, Dad, the Chrysler is making a noise. I think something is wrong with the muffler."

We finished eating and walked out to the car. Dad got down on one knee and glanced underneath. He stood up and looked me squarely in the eye. "Son, did you turn off

the switch, mash the gas and then turn the car back on?"

I stared down at the ground as my face reddened. Honesty, I decided, was the best policy. "Yes, sir," I grunted, embarrassed.

Dad was a hard-as-nails Navy veteran known for his hot temper. I waited for an explosion, knowing it would dwarf my car's backfire and probably end my days of carefree driving. Instead, he smiled and said, "I thought so. I did the same thing in a '27 Ford. Don't do it again."

We got the muffler fixed, and Dad never mentioned it to Mom. More important than what I learned about mufflers was that my dad had a sense of humor and realized what it was like to be a teenager. Best of all, it was the beginning of a change in our relationship that lasted the rest of his life.

SIDNEY HEPLER · SUNRISE, FL

Sidney hoped to impress his girlfriend, Linda, with the '46 Chrysler's performance.

OVERSEAS TRAVEL

Auto imports cruise right into the American market.

1964 »

Snug as a Bug

Volkswagen sold just two cars in the U.S. in 1949, but sales rose steadily until peaking at 570,000 in 1970. Symbolizing hippie counterculture didn't hurt. An alternative to Detroit's big-engine giants, the VW Bug was distinctive from the start and changed very little— making it easy to maintain year over year, as this ad points out.

« 1962

Lost in Translation

Though French Renaults were sold in the U.S. as early as the mid-'50s, the brand struggled, despite boasting innovations like four-wheel disc brakes, child-safe locks, and high gas mileage, as this ad touts. Renault had some success in the 1970s in a partnership with American Motors, but by the mid-'80s, the market for its cars had mostly evaporated.

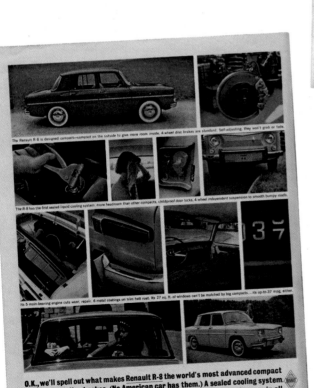

Michelle was that friend everyone counted on to be the driver.

Charger Gave Her the Muscle She Wanted

She was thrilled to get her brother's hand-me-down.

The love of muscle cars is definitely in my genes, passed down to my older brother, Eric, and me from our dad.

When I was 18, Eric sold me his car, a 1974 Dodge Charger. Hands down, this black beauty was always my favorite car. Cruising around the streets in this classic was pure joy. The car was a real head-turner, as not many of them were on the road in my hometown of Brockton in 1985.

The history of the car's purchase was part of what made it so special. Dad worked in a family-owned paint store on Newbury Street in Boston. When the owner's son announced he was selling his car, Dad instantly tuned in because he wanted to get the car for Eric, who was then a few months away from getting his license.

The asking price was a bit steep. But one night, the guys from the paint store went out for a few drinks after work. As spirits lightened, the price of the car dropped to $700! The next thing I knew, it was parked in our driveway. Eric sat behind the wheel every day, waiting for the moment he'd be old enough to get his driver's license.

The car was still in excellent condition after a couple of years, but Eric was ready to move on to an even better sports car. He wasn't sad about parting with the Charger, as I was in need of some wheels. Eric gave me a family discount, and so I became the proud owner of this classic.

Among my friends, I was the oldest, and I was the first to get my license. As a result, I became the driver of the group, always picking up my friends for school and taking them on many fun trips to Nantasket Beach. Whenever I reflect on the days of my youth, I recall cruising around in the Charger, with Tom Petty blaring through the stereo speakers.

MICHELLE MARVEL · BROCKTON, MA

Sally Revamps Cornish Holidays

In rainy U.K., glamping is the way to go.

W hen my children were young I decided to take them camping in Cornwall, so I bought a tent and the many items needed to camp in rainy England. It was a bit of a nightmare holiday, and after that I vowed I'd never sleep in a tent again: If I ever went back, it was going to be in an Airstream or a van.

I've always loved cars, specifically vintage, so the only option for me was something unique and old. I looked online and in magazines for a perfect fit and found this little gem, complete with original converted Devon camper interior. It was a 1967 Volkswagen Split Screen 21 Window Microbus/Samba. We called it Sally.

I purchased our Sally in 2005 in Birmingham with its original engine. Unfortunately it broke down on the way back to London. After getting it—on a trailer—to a specialist garage in the city, we decided to replace the engine with a 2-liter flat-four for more power. The previous owner had upgraded the suspension and braking system to disc brakes on the front, while leaving the original drum brakes on the rear.

In 2016 Sally underwent a thorough, bare-metal restoration to get rid of all of the normal rust issues and prepare for a fresh paint job. It also got all-new electrics, a replacement roof and power steering, which vastly improved the driving experience.

The vehicle is now in brilliant condition, but my children are grown so I'm hoping to sell it. We spent many wonderful years camping in Sally and a vintage 1952 Airstream, which I purchased to sit alongside her.

MARK HUTCHINSON · LONDON, ENGLAND

Iowa Boy Is Teenage Whiz Kid

His love of sports set the wheels in motion.

O ur farm near Holstein, Iowa, was about 6 miles from town. I attended high school in the late '40s and early '50s, and the only transportation there and back was the school bus.

I really wanted to play sports—football, track and basketball—which were held after school. Of course, if I rode the bus, there was no way for me to do sports. In the 1940s my parents had very little money to spend on things like transportation. My dad told me I was going to have to find my own way to get home if I wanted to start playing sports after school.

I would have to make some money, so I took jobs helping the neighbors so I could buy something to ride. I chose a Whizzer motorbike. The Gambles store in Holstein sold them for around $175. I eventually made enough to buy a bike.

I rode the bike to school every day, even in winter. Once it snowed so much that I had to leave the bike at school and catch a ride home. Until I graduated in 1952, I had a reliable way to get to and from school, and I got to play sports because of the Whizzer motorbike.

BILL WEBER · TUCSON, AZ

Bill had room for his neighbor, Arlene, on the Whizzer.

RED WING MOTORCYCLE CLUB
1940

MICHIGAN STATE FAIRGROUNDS
DETROIT, MICHIGAN

Gary didn't know his parents were in a riding club. Dolores is fourth from the left; Lee is the tall guy just left of center, behind the Harley-Davidson.

Born To Ride

An old photo reveals the road to love and marriage.

M y wife, Dorothea, and I met 35 years ago. Our relationship blossomed partly because we shared an interest in motorcycle riding. While raising five children, we kept riding and joined a national, family-oriented motorcycle club. We rode locally in Michigan and around the country.

Our bikes were large and quiet, with intercoms in the helmets and radios to communicate with our fellow riders. On long trips, we pulled a matching trailer to carry everything that the on-board storage wouldn't allow.

During Michigan's short riding season, we often joined our group on Sundays for dinner. In the off-season, we gathered weekly in the evenings to dine and talk about riding.

One night, our friend Jim shared an old photo of a bike club. The riders, pictured at the Michigan State Fairgrounds, were dressed in uniforms of the late 1930s. The photo was inscribed "Red Wing Motorcycle Club 1940." I'd heard of the club, which is still active today.

We passed the photo around, and I looked closely at a tall figure in the middle. Something about him looked familiar—I realized it was my dad! Dorothea took a look, and after examining the women's faces, said, "And isn't that your mother?" There she was, fourth from the left, together with Dad in a picture we never knew existed.

Luckily I was able to ask my father, Lee, about the photo, and he told us a story that started in the same way as ours.

We learned that over 75 years ago he and my mother, Dolores, shared an interest in motorcycle riding. They were married in 1941, the year after the photo was taken. But World War II and, later, demands of raising a large family kept them from pursuing their hobby. Dad helped us label almost all the people in the photo. We shared copies with my five brothers and two sisters, and now that Dad is gone, we are grateful for the keepsake.

Dorothea and I still deeply love motorcycles, but our motor home has taken priority for road trips these days. When we travel, our beloved Honda scooter still comes along with us on a carrier, and once we park the rig and unload the bike, we can still "get in the wind."

GARY SCHUBRING · CHESTERFIELD, MI

BEN MARTIN/GETTY IMAGES

PONY RIDE
A family rides in a Mustang convertible inside Ford Motor Co.'s pavilion at the 1964 World's Fair in Queens, NY. Outside, others queue up for their own quick trip in the new muscle car model.

DRIVING DOWN MEMORY LANE

FAMILY OUTING

I was 3 and ready to go for a drive in my brother Al's convertible near Cottage Grove, Minnesota, in 1960. Lyle is up front, and Dale and Uncle Frank are in the back seat.
SALLY LEE • ST. MICHAEL, MN

TOGETHER AT LAST

I began my love affair with the red coupe in the 1940s, when one of my neighbors' cars caught my eye. When I started restoring pre-World War II cars in the '80s, I kept an eye out for those wheels that made my heart sing—and I found my dream ride less than 100 miles from home.
GERALD ELWOOD
BUCYRUS, KS

RIGHT: COURTESY OF TOYOTA MOTOR CORPORATION

CROWN JEWELS

Toyopet Crowns from Toyota Motors are loaded for shipping to the United States after the Japanese automaker set up its American headquarters in California in 1957. Fewer than 300 of those first imports sold and are collectors' items today.

Karen ignored the naysayers, looking instead to family and friends for tools and advice to overhaul her '53 Ford Mainline.

A Woman's Place Is Under the Hood

"No" was just a bump in the road.

M y wife, Karen, was raised by her mother, Gladys Clayton; Karen's father abandoned them when she was 11. Money was tight, and they depended on each other in every circumstance of their lives.

She and her mom took the bus everywhere, but when Karen turned 16, they decided to get a car. As a student at Cleveland Heights High School in 1958, Karen thought she would be able to take the auto shop class in order to to learn how to repair a fixer-upper. However, she wasn't allowed to sign up, since there was no place for girls to change clothes for class.

Karen enlisted the help of a mechanic she referred to only as Amil, who worked at the local Pure Oil gas station. Amil helped Karen secure a 1953 Ford Mainline sedan that needed its engine replaced, and he took her to the junkyard to buy a used Ford flathead V-8. Once the car was dropped off in her driveway, she used the garage door to rig a chain hoist, thus beginning her adventures in auto mechanics.

Karen had spent summers in Tunkhannock, Pennsylvania, with her aunt and uncle, who owned a Sinclair gas station. She'd pumped gas, checked oil, changed tires and learned simple mechanics by watching her uncle. Now she worked on her own car as Amil lent tools and gave advice on solving the many problems Karen encountered while trying to make this derelict car functional again.

The neighborhood boys ridiculed her as she worked to revive the dead beast. Determined, Karen pursued her dream. Finally the day came to fire up the car, and to her joy—and the surprise of the neighborhood—the engine coughed to life. Karen and her mom had wheels for the first time.

To celebrate, she drove the old car to school and right up to the door of the shop she had been forbidden from entering. Soon after, she and her mother made the 360-mile trip from Cleveland to Tunkhannock to show her uncle and aunt what she'd been able to do, thanks to their support and continued encouragement.

JIM SKINNER · SEBRING, OH

Joyrider

This photo from 1920 shows my excitement when Grandpa Cobb let me sit behind the wheel of his car. He was a doctor, and he used the vehicle for his job—and for making his granddaughter smile.

JANE LANE · NORTH FORT MEYERS, FL

CHAPTER 8

FOR THE LOVE OF THE GAME

Young fans come face to face
with the heroes and legends
of their favorite pastimes.

Angels in the Outfield

While growing up in New Jersey in the '60s, I went to as many Yankee games as I could. One time dad took me, my sister and my cousin to see our beloved Bronx Bombers. Our seats at field level gave me the opportunity to meet Jimmy Piersall, who played for the Angels.

RUSSELL MARCHETTA · NOKOMIS, FL

Players' Conference Off the Field

A baseball fan gets the inside scoop from a legend.

My friend Randy Story and I were at a restaurant in West Plains, Missouri, when he nudged me. "There's Preacher," he said, referring to pitcher Preacher Roe, who played with the St. Louis Cardinals, the Pittsburgh Pirates and the Brooklyn Dodgers from 1938 to 1954.

Randy was a teacher at West Plains schools, and Roe's son was on the school board. Randy had met him before and knew of my affinity for baseball history. We debated about interrupting Roe's dinner. I knew that I might anger him, but I also knew this was a once-in-a-lifetime chance to talk baseball with one of the greats.

So we barged in on the former player's meal.

Roe was gracious and seemed appreciative that someone remembered his career. I asked him about his Brooklyn days playing with Jackie Robinson and the rivalry between his team and the New York Yankees. After that, I steered the conversation to that amazing moment in 1951.

That was the year Roe won 22 games and lost only three, leading Brooklyn to a tie with the New York Giants in the National League. On Oct. 3, 1951, after the teams split two playoff games, the Dodgers were leading 4-2.

The Giants had two runners on base in the bottom of the ninth in the deciding game for the

From left: Thomson's homer capped an incredible rally for the Giants; Preacher Roe wore down batters with his precise pitching control; budding baseball historian Kenneth Heard at home in Pittsburgh, PA, in 1962.

National League pennant when Bobby Thomson came to bat. Roe sat in the bullpen when the Dodgers called on reliever Ralph Branca to pitch to Thomson. Fans know what happened next.

Thomson hit a home run, giving the Giants the victory 5-4, and announcer Russ Hodges went nuts with his cry over and over, "The Giants win the pennant! The Giants win the pennant!"

I could tell, more than 55 years later, that homer still bothered Preacher Roe. He said he knew the ball was a home run, despite its low trajectory. "It was hit so hard and low, I thought it would knock the fence over," he said. He was sure the Giants stole Branca's signs, so Thomson knew a fastball

was coming. Roe's claim was substantiated in Joshua Prager's *The Echoing Green* (2006), which details the Giants' system involving a telescope and a buzzer to relay stolen signs to their batters.

My father, Edmund, grew up in New York in the 1940s in the days of Yogi Berra and Joe DiMaggio and was a huge baseball fan. My obsession with baseball history didn't really take off until after my dad died. He had stories about the game that I would love to hear now, but I'll always treasure my talk with Roe, who died a short time later.

KENNETH HEARD · JONESBORO, AR

I knew I might anger him, but it was a lifetime chance to talk baseball with one of the greats. So we barged in on the former player's meal.

SITTING PRETTY
The St. Louis Browns pose in 1944 after winning the city's only American League pennant. They beat the New York Yankees to clinch the championship, but they lost the World Series to their rivals across town, the Cardinals, in the so-called "streetcar series."

Worth the Price of Admission

A trip to see the "real Yankees" didn't disappoint.

——

Baseball was huge in our Oklahoma town. The minor league teams for the Dodgers and Cardinals played there twice, and Dizzy Dean spent a couple of preseason games there, too. Giants pitcher Carl Hubbell grew up a few miles away, as did the Waner brothers, Lloyd and Paul, who played for the Pirates. I was a Dodgers fan, and my little brother, Jerry, picked the Yankees as his favorite. Considering fellow Oklahoman Mickey Mantle was in his prime, it was an easy choice.

We watched major league games on TV, but seeing those teams in their far-off cities was the stuff of dreams. In June 1959, Daddy took us to Kansas City to see the "real" Yankees: Mickey Mantle, Whitey Ford, Moose Skowron, Yogi Berra and the others. They were playing the Athletics before teams began to move west—the Dodgers to Los Angeles, the Giants to San Francisco and the A's to San Diego.

It was a big trip, and Daddy spared no expense. He installed an air conditioner in our '56 Buick and we got to stay in a motel. We were at the park before the gates even opened. Our mezzanine seats were right behind home plate, and there he was—Mickey Mantle. He came to bat in the first inning and hit a home run! Daddy stood up. "Let's go," he said. "We've seen what came to see." We were startled, but Daddy grinned and sat down.

I wondered years later if I had remembered accurately that Mantle hit another home run and a triple. When it became possible to check things via the internet, I did just that. I didn't imagine it: That's really what happened.

I've been to dozens of games since then, and even saw a World Series. But in one of the last conversations I had with Jerry, we agreed nothing came close to that game in 1959.

ANN McDONALD · SHAWNEE, OK

The Kansas City Athletics hosted the New York Yankees at the 30,000-seat Municipal Stadium. Opened in 1923, the stadium held the first Negro League World Series in 1924. It was torn down in 1976.

Hank Aaron of the Milwaukee Braves makes a running catch into the ivy off a drive by Chicago Cubs first baseman Dale Long at Wrigley Field in June 1958.

MEMORIES OF SEEING THE IVY ARE EVERGREEN

MY PARENTS HAD FOUR SONS.
Our dad was the sole provider while Mom stayed at home; her job was taking care of the family. Money was tight, but on a special occasion in 1966, my dad took me, the oldest, and my brother Mike, who is 11 months younger than me, to a Chicago Cubs game at Wrigley Field. Our brother Tom was too young and little Bill hadn't been born yet.

Dad got the only seats he could afford—in the cheapest area, known as the nosebleed section. Concessions were a luxury, so Mike and I split a hot dog and small Coke. But we had a blast watching the Cubs and just being at Wrigley.

Fast forward to 1980: I was 23, single, and had just started my sales career. My kid brother Bill was 11 years old. Remembering my own experiences at the ballpark, I thought it would be fun to take him to a Cubs game so he could enjoy the same thrill I had at his age. We sat in the bleachers and got there early for batting practice. Unlike when I went to Wrigley as a child, I let Bill eat as many hot dogs and other concessions, and drink as many Cokes, as he wanted.

Though Bill went home with a stomachache, the highlight of the day—other than seeing the Cubs defeat the Montreal Expos—came during batting practice. Ellis Valentine of the Expos sent a fly ball out to the left-field bleachers, and my kid brother caught it in his baseball cap. I can still see the smile on his face 40 years later.

STEVEN AINSWORTH • WEST DUNDEE, IL

Salvatore never forgot the details of his meeting with his idol Gil Hodges, right.

MEETING THE BIG GUY

FEW PEOPLE HAD CARS when I was growing up in Bensonhurst, Brooklyn, and the streets had plenty of room for ballgames: There was stoopball, triangle ball, handball and stickball. And baseball.

I loved going to Ebbets Field, the home of the Dodgers since 1913. The Dodgers were a team of great, lovable players, and when I could scrape the money together, off to Ebbets Field I would go.

It was a simple ballpark—some would call it a bandbox—but memorable things happened there in the early '50s. Usually I went with friends, but sometimes with my father, or even alone.

My idol was Gil Hodges. Gil had a reputation for not saying much, never arguing with umpires, and being an all-around gentleman. When he went into a hitting slump, prayers were solicited for him in most pulpits in Brooklyn.

The Dodgers sponsored a pregame TV show, Happy Felton's *Knothole Gang*. A Dodgers player gave wide-eyed kids tips on catching grounders, hitting or bunting.

It was held in a corner of right field, and the boys were picked out of the crowd, usually from the grandstand. I never was able to get a grandstand seat because it cost too much, but an usher from my neighborhood would sometimes let me sneak in under the turnstile when the coast was clear.

One day, I managed to get in. The opponents must have been the Chicago Cubs, the Cincinnati Reds or the Pittsburgh Pirates—teams that took turns being in last place, so not too many people went to see them.

The player giving tips that day was Gil Hodges. I had never seen him up close. He was big, with hands that could crush a melon and arms like a blacksmith. And to top off this perfect day, another player trotted up and said hi. That player was Jackie Robinson.

SALVATORE BARCIA · LEVITTOWN, NY

Red-Hot for the Red Sox

Their place was a slice of Heaven near Kenmore Square.

Back in the mid-1950s and the early 1960s, I lived with my grandmother in an apartment at the Hotel Buckminster, which is practically across the street from the hallowed Fenway Park in Boston, Massachusetts. For a preteen girl and baseball fan, game day in Boston was always exciting. Crowds would spill out of the Kenmore subway station and make their way to the stadium.

The food vendors and pennant sellers lined Boylston Street, vying for customers, shouting their wares in classic Beantown accents: "Get yer red-hots heah!" "Pennants, souvenirs heah!"

My grandmother and I would enjoy watching the spectacle from our apartment. When the game was on, we could tell when something good happened because the cheers of the crowd were very intense. When a Red Sox player hit a home run, windows in the buildings next to the park rattled from the roaring. The lights from the night games lit up our bedroom and kept us awake, but we didn't care—the yelling fans wouldn't have allowed us to sleep anyway. Ted Williams was our hero.

The best part of living so close to the famous park was being able to sneak up to our roof and look over into the stadium. I had my own private viewing stand and loved every minute, as long as no one found me up there. To this day, I cherish the memories I have of Fenway—of feeling part of something special. When I see aerial shots of Boston, the hotel and the stadium, I'm reminded again how lucky I was to have had a front-row seat to a magical time in baseball history.

ELAINE BUTLER · NEVADA CITY, CA

Lolly Hopkins of Providence, RI, above, a devoted Boston fan, graced Fenway with her trusty megaphone in the '30s, '40s and '50s.

Below: John and Tony did what brothers do—go to ballgames, eat peanuts and occasionally disagree on the finer points of a story. Right: Three Rivers.

A Day at the Park

Brothers and Pirates fans strike out on their own.

In the summer of 1970, Three Rivers Stadium, home of the Pittsburgh Pirates, had just opened and my brother and I wanted to see a game.

I was 13, and Tony, 11. We hopped on the bus, the airport flyer, which took us from our east end neighborhood directly to the ballpark.

We wound our way through the stadium until we located our seats in the far reaches of the upper deck. There we sat, eating peanuts and Cracker Jack, enjoying the game—until Manny Sanguillen, the Pirates catcher, hit a broken-bat single.

I grabbed Tony's hand.

"C'mon," I said. "I'm going to get that bat."

Around and around we went to the other end of the cavernous park, until at last we arrived at the first-class seats next to the Pirates' dugout. There we saw pitcher Doc Ellis pacing back and forth, bat handle in hand.

"Hey, Doc!" I yelled. "Can I have that?"

Now this is where my version of the story differs from Tony's.

Tony always said that Doc joked, "Give me five dollars first" before handing me the bat handle. I don't remember that part.

I do recall just about everything else from that day, however. I still have that bat handle and I still love baseball.

Most of all, even though my brother has passed away, I will always cherish that day and all the days we spent together growing up in Pittsburgh.

JOHN MAGGIO · PITTSBURGH, PA

I still have that bat handle and I still love baseball.

VINTAGE ADS · VINTAGE ADS

BEST IN THE GAME

These colorful ads promised athletes the glory of victory.

1951 »

Made with Florida Sunshine

Encouraging its readers to drink two glasses a day, this ad for fresh-frozen orange juice uses Robin Roberts to tout the drink's high vitamin C content and health benefits. One "little can" made four whole glasses!

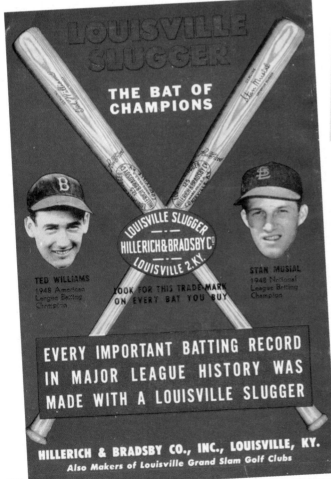

« 1958

Swinging for the Fences

One of the most iconic brands in baseball, Louisville Slugger got its start in 1884 and today produces nearly 2 million bats each year. This ad, featuring legends Stan Musial and Ted Williams, encouraged its readers to "look for the trademark" oval-shaped brand on every bat purchased.

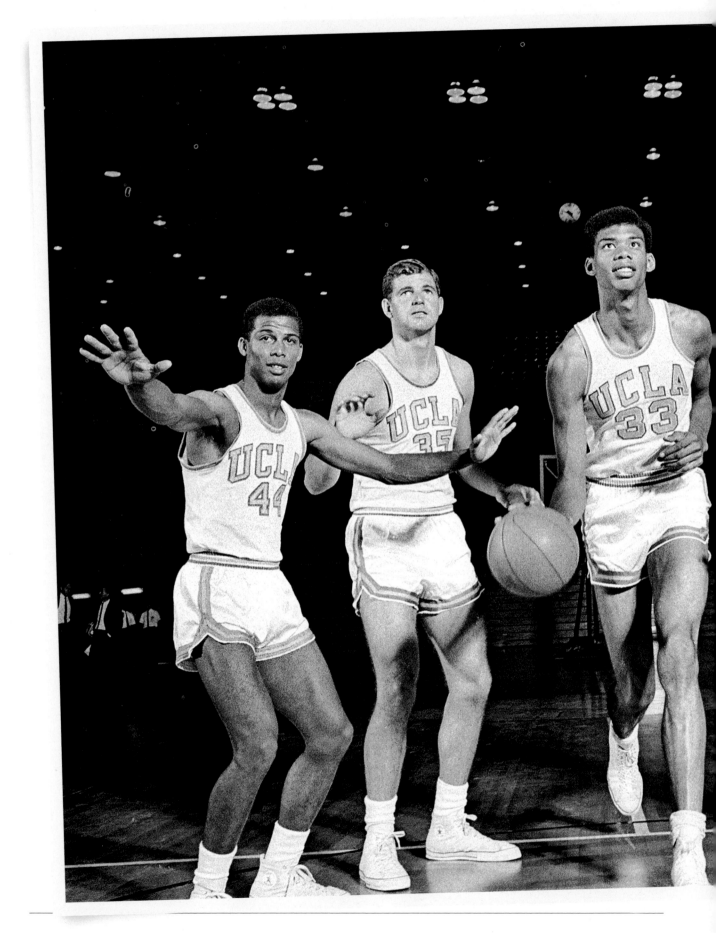

FUTURE'S SO BRIGHT
Lew Alcindor (33) leads a
UCLA practice at the start
of the 1966-'67 season, just
as the Bruins' began an
unparalleled run to seven
straight NCAA men's
basketball championships.
Alcindor played most of
his professional career as
Kareem Abdul-Jabbar.

Historic Moments

These athletes, and their iconic victories, left a lasting legacy in the world of sports.

GAME, SET, MATCH

Americans Jimmy Connors and Chris Evert show off their shiny championship trophies for the men's and women's singles titles at Wimbledon in July 1974.

"THE GOAL"

Bobby Orr flies through the air after scoring in sudden-death overtime against the St. Louis Blues, clinching the Stanley Cup for the Boston Bruins on May 10, 1970. Known in Boston simply as "The Goal," this moment is shown in a bronze statue by the former Boston Garden.

A NEW RECORD
With a $200 custom boot on his toeless right foot, New Orleans Saints kicker Tom Dempsey nails a record 63-yard field goal for the win against the heavily favored Detroit Lions at Tulane Stadium on Nov. 8, 1970.

TWO TITLES
Arthur Ashe poses after winning the men's singles final at the U.S. Amateur Championships at Longwood Cricket Club in Chestnut Hill, MA, in August 1968. Two weeks later, he won the U.S. Open, making him the first and only man to win both titles in the same year.

On TV with Joe DiMaggio

The kid throws a game to win a better prize.

O n Oct. 5, 1952, I was invited to appear as a guest on a TV show hosted by Joe DiMaggio, one of my baseball heroes. The program, called *The Buitoni Show*, was sponsored by that big pasta company.

I was one of three baseball players selected to go on the show. We were all 14 and students at the American Baseball Academy, which was free to boys 13-18 who had an interest in baseball and lived in New York City. The academy was founded by Phil Rizzuto, the Yankees shortstop, and professional baseball players instructed students.

That week's show had a guest appearance by Rizzuto, who was the maestro of bunting in the American League. On the show he was going to teach the three of us the art of bunting.

I recall DiMaggio was dressed impeccably in a blue pinstriped suit, with his gray hair shining in the bright set lights. We were supposed to answer baseball trivia questions, and the winner would be awarded a Bulova watch. The runner-up would win a year's supply of Buitoni spaghetti.

I made it to the final question, which was, "Who pitched the most scoreless innings in the World Series?" I knew the player was Babe Ruth. But as I thought about the prizes and asked myself what I would rather win, the answer was easy. So I said, "Whitey Ford."

To a 14-year-old, when time seemed endless, spaghetti for a year was better than a watch. I'm sure I looked more happy than sad when Joe said, "Sorry, Ron. You win a year's supply of spaghetti."

For the next year, a delivery of Buitoni pasta arrived at our apartment each and every month, right on schedule.

To this day my twin daughters, Serena and Vinica, and I eat a serving of Buitoni at least once a week, prepared by Patricia, my wife of 44 years.

RON WEISS · HIGHLAND FALLS, NY

To a 14-year-old, when time seemed endless, spaghetti for a year was better than a watch.

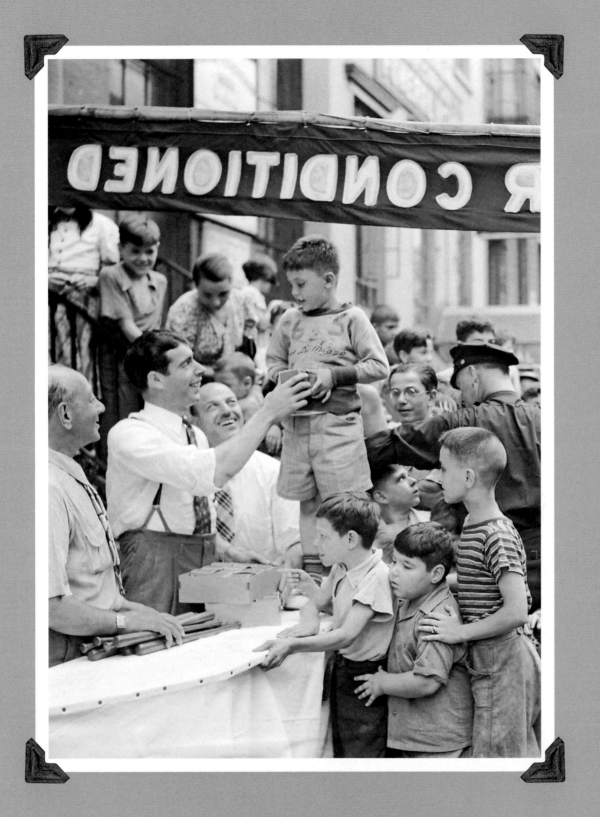

A Hit with the Kids

The Yankees' Joe DiMaggio gives a baseball to Frankie Camerano, 6, at an event in New York's Greenwich Village in 1941. Frankie has 56 on both shoulders of his shirt in honor of Joltin' Joe's unrivaled hitting streak.

CHAPTER 9

SEEING
STARS

Encounters with celebrities illuminate
the humans behind the fame.

"Over Here, Mr. Sinatra!"

Frank Sinatra stands on a stepladder to sign autographs amid
a sea of fans in Los Angeles in 1943.

The youthful Rolling Stones, with their shaggy hair and informal suits, were unknown in Omaha in 1964.

Not Your Father's Blues Band

She was there for the Rolling Stones' early days.

————

Music was always coming from inside our house. When not in the fields or feeding livestock on our farm near Little Sioux, Iowa, we all listened to the radio or record player. My father favored gospel and blues. My mother liked the Big Band sound. My two older sisters loved Elvis. And I, a high school sophomore, looked across the Atlantic to the Beatles.

My friend Katie called me early one Saturday in June 1964 to invite me to the big city of Omaha, Nebraska, to see a local weekly TV show called *Dancestand*. "There's some English group called the Rolling Stones," Katie said. "No one has heard of them, but they have an album. They're playing tonight at the auditorium."

Katie's older sister, Nancy, had just landed a secretarial job at the station. Nancy's job was to make sure the bleachers were filled in the TV studio, so Katie's mom drove us and Katie's cousins to Omaha. After consulting with my parents— "Rolling Stones? That's an old blues song," my dad said—all was set.

At the studio, a disheveled studio manager with headphones and a clipboard briefed us. "When I point at you, scream!" There were only about 20

Resa's room was decorated with Rolling Stones posters and a state-of-the-art record player.

of us, and it looked as if everyone had called their daughters, sisters and cousins to make up the audience. The manager added, "Scream like you're really happy to be here."

On a circular stage were five young men with unmatched clothing and shaggy hair that almost covered their eyes and ears. Two of them, Bill Wyman and Keith Richards, sported vests. Only the drummer, Charlie Watts, wore a tie. The small audience chatted about them, agreeing that they looked nothing like the Beatles. The band members seemed as curious about us as we were about them. They smiled at us, and we giggled and waved back.

The boys checked their guitars and speakers and talked among themselves as they watched six women dancing together to the Beach Boys' "I Get Around" in another part of the cramped studio.

The show's host faced the camera and held up the band's first album. "On our stage today— and appearing at the auditorium tonight—are England's newest hit-makers, the Rolling Stones!"

The stage manager pointed at us, and we screamed. Some of the girls even put their hands up to their faces and jumped up and down in their seats as they had seen Beatles fans do on TV.

Then Brian Jones pulled a harmonica from his jacket pocket, and the Rolling Stones sang their first American single, "Not Fade Away." Mick Jagger moved fast as a hummingbird, sliding and dancing sideways on one foot, and all the while singing and shaking two sets of maracas.

When the song ended, the host interviewed the group, asking each band member his name. They politely responded and shook hands with the host, who said, "Tell us about your concert tonight." Keith responded, "I would if I knew where I was." It wasn't drugs or rock 'n' roll that prompted his answer: The group was in the States for only two weeks, and they honestly didn't know how large it was in comparison to England.

Not missing a beat, the host asked the next question: "What do you like about the United States?" The young Brits chuckled a bit, and replied almost in unison, "The girls!" True,

unpracticed screams of excitement came up from the small audience.

One of the show's sponsors was a local car dealership, and a Mustang convertible was parked next to the stage for the commercial break. One by one, following Mick, the band members went to look over the convertible. Mick climbed into the driver's seat; Brian sat beside him. Charlie, Bill and Keith walked around the car admiring it.

The host, trying to keep his cool, strolled over and took the keys out of the convertible. As he looked at the camera, he intoned, "We'll be right back after these words from our sponsors." I'm not sure if the viewing audience heard it or not, but the studio audience heard him: "OK, boys, get away from the car!"

After that, I never left the Rolling Stones. I've attended as many of their concerts as possible, when family, career and finances didn't intervene. Among fans, it is common practice to state how many times you've seen them. When the bragging starts, all I have to say is, "Omaha, 1964." Everyone gets quiet.

How unpredictable life is. Brian died in 1969 and Bill left the band in 1992, but the Rolling Stones still rock the world. They completed their "No Filter" tour of North America in Miami in August 2019. Yes, 55 years later, I was there.

RESA WILLIS · WILLARD, MO

Jazz Diplomacy

Louis Armstrong spread the message of music.

———

When I was 16, I met one of my musical heroes—Louis Armstrong, one of the all-time greats of jazz.

The occasion was a concert given by Louis Armstrong & His All-Stars on Nov. 24, 1956, at Muhlenberg College in Allentown, Pennsylvania.

A junior at nearby Whitehall High School, I was sports editor of the school newspaper. Our faculty adviser knew I was into jazz and suggested that I interview Armstrong. My dad was active in many civic associations and knew the sponsors of the concert, so I was granted access to the band's dressing room.

My favorite of Armstrong's albums was one he made a year earlier. Called *Ambassador Satch*, it was recorded in 1955 in Europe while Armstrong and his band were touring as cultural diplomats for the U.S. State Department. Showing how long he'd been making records, one of the songs on that album was a revival of "West End Blues," which he first recorded to great acclaim in 1928.

I started my interview by saying, "Mr. Armstrong, I want to tell you that I'm collecting your records and I've been a fan of yours for a long time."

He gave me a big smile and said simply, "Thank you, Daddy."

He talked about his early career, and also told me he hoped to play in Russia. He said he never took vacations, and just wanted to make music.

Meanwhile, my dad spotted a professional photographer he knew and talked him into taking a picture of me with Armstrong.

My interview and the picture ran on the front page of the school paper.

DON CHARLES · SUWANEE, GA

High school student Don Charles with the legendary jazz artist in 1956.

Ringing in 1996 with the famous newsman in Vienna made for the trip of a lifetime for one longtime fan.

Second Impression

Walter Cronkite was always working, even on vacation.

On the two separate vacations I encountered Walter Cronkite, there was no such thing as selfies, so I don't have photos with him. But both meetings gave me memories that I cherish.

The first time we met was in 1995 at the Imperial Hotel in Vienna, Austria. My husband, Hank, surprised me with a trip to celebrate our 25th wedding anniversary and my 60th birthday. Hank had taken note of a group trip to Vienna that I learned about in a travel class, and unbeknownst to me, he signed us up for a weeklong fantasy trip.

Hank and I attended the famous New Year's performance in the Musikverein concert hall during that visit. The hall is next to the Imperial Hotel. Zubin Mehta was the conductor that year and Cronkite was the host.

After the concert our tour group headed into the hotel's private dining room, and I found myself standing next to Cronkite at a table heaped full of marvelous desserts. We discussed which ones to take, and just how many of them it would be acceptable to pile onto our plates, before wishing one another a happy new year and returning to our respective tables.

Three years later, Hank and I were in a lodge at Yellowstone National Park. We saw Cronkite surrounded by family in the dining room, and our server told us that he had just completed narrating a documentary. The next morning, while awaiting Old Faithful's eruption, I was in the hotel's lobby when a smiling Cronkite walked toward me. I seized the opportunity to say hi, and I reminded him of our Vienna encounter.

During this meeting my husband was buying postcards in the gift shop. He saw me talking with someone and wondered who it was. Upon coming closer, he immediately recognized it was none other than Walter Cronkite.

We talked with him about his recently published autobiography, which we had listened to on tape during our drive to Yellowstone. He was genuinely curious and thoroughly interested in our comments about his work.

BARBARA BERNS · PALM CITY, FL

A shining star in the golden age of Hollywood, Grant perfected an air of refinement, even when meeting his biggest fans.

Cary Grant's Line Had Three Little Words

But he was a master at delivering it.

As a young New England transplant, I relocated to Manhattan after graduating from college. I wore out more than a few pairs of leather pumps in pursuit of a career in the Big Apple until I finally secured an interview with the Fabergé company on Fifth Avenue.

I was sitting in the reception area when who should exit the elevator but Cary Grant. He was on the board of directors as a brand ambassador for the cosmetics line, and his appearance had every female in the vicinity rubbernecking to not only get a good look at him, but also to hear that recognizable voice. With his impeccable posture, shock of white hair and thick black glasses, Mr. Grant exuded that remarkable quality very few possess—he could actually make a person swoon.

He disappeared into the inner offices. After my appointment, I was waiting for the elevator when Mr. Grant emerged and stood next to me. He held out his hand to prevent the door from closing, looked at me and said, "After you, dear."

The two of us got on the elevator—what a thrill to travel 20 floors alone with Cary Grant! Neither one of us uttered a word.

In the lobby, again Mr. Grant held the elevator door open and said, "After you, dear." We walked through the lobby to the doors leading to Fifth Avenue, and again he held the heavy glass door and said, "After you, dear." Gobsmacked, I watched him get into his waiting car. He turned and gave me a big smile and a wink.

I immediately ran to a phone booth and called my mother. When I relayed the delightful details of my extraordinary encounter, I'm certain she swooned, too! To this day, when I watch a Cary Grant film, I remember his three words just for me, "After you, dear!"

EILEEN CASEY · MOUNT PLEASANT, SC

On the Campaign Trail With Shirley Temple Black

The former star stood up for women.

During the 1960s, I was active in the San Mateo, California, Young Republicans. This was when Barry Goldwater ran for president and Ronald Reagan was elected governor of California. One of my favorites among people I met during those years was Shirley Temple Black, the former child movie star, who lived with her husband, Charles Black, in the hills of San Mateo County.

My mother had been a big fan of Shirley Temple and told me a lot about her and her films when I was growing up. The star I met in about 1966 was almost 40, soft-spoken and fun, still flashing her famous dimples.

She ran for the Republican nomination—the press called her Mrs. Shirley Temple Black—for a seat in the U.S. House of Representatives. Her goal was "to break the all-male hold on California's congressional seats." Though favored, she lost to Paul McCloskey, a decorated Korean War vet who took an antiwar stance. Reports at the time said that many Democrats crossed party lines to vote in the open primary election.

Then I decided to run for the leadership of the San Mateo Young Republicans. Shirley was happy to support a female candidate and posed with me for a publicity photo. Gender aside, I was the best qualified, and right up until the election, no one opposed me.

Sadly, in the end, my campaign went no better than Shirley's. At our annual meeting in January 1968, male students from Stanford decided they didn't want a woman as chairman, and they quickly formed a coalition with two other all-male delegations to defeat me with a male candidate they nominated from the floor.

I went on to manage a congressional campaign and spent a summer working in Washington, D.C., but I didn't end up pursuing a career in politics. I became a lawyer.

BRENDA KIMSEY WARNEKA · LAUGHLIN, NV

This publicity still for her election campaign in 1968 showed Brenda, left, with Shirley Temple Black.

VINTAGE ADS · VINTAGE ADS

BOX OFFICE BONANZA

Movie thrills from 70 years ago.

Better Dead Than Red

Exploiting postwar fears of the "red menace" with the subtlety of an anvil, this movie was garden-variety blackmail drama dressed up as thriller. The title was such a buzzkill that RKO changed it to *The Woman on Pier 13* a year later.

Welcome to the Dark Side

Despite its billing as the "biggest picture in 10 years," *Black Magic* has been eclipsed since by Orson Welles' more famous 1949 film, *The Third Man*. That's a shame, because he's truly mesmerizing as a hypnotist plotting revenge on the man who killed his parents.

 Paris When It Sizzles

Charles Laughton plays a French detective hunting a contract killer through the streets of Paris, leading to a nail-biting chase up the city's most famous landmark. Director Burgess Meredith, who also stars, later said the location shots were grueling, with cast members suffering from vertigo by the time filming ended.

Everyone Wants to Be In His Neighborhood

In a busy airport, Mr. Rogers takes time to be himself.

Flying to visit my sister in California in 1988, my flight had a layover in Pittsburgh. While waiting at the gate for my connecting flight, I noticed people whispering excitedly and pointing toward the escalator. I immediately recognized the cause: Everyone's friend, Mr. Rogers, was stepping off the escalator.

It was heartwarming to watch him stop and talk to all who waved or said hello. I'm sure he was anxious to get to his destination, but in true Fred Rogers fashion, he took time to acknowledge those around him. He shook hands with each adult and stooped down to the level of each child and talked for as long as every child wanted. Each interaction included his warm smile and his full attention.

As a huge Mr. Rogers fan, I couldn't pass up this opportunity. Not wanting to take time away from any child, I waited till the crowd around him had thinned before I approached. I shook his hand and explained that as a preschool teacher I appreciated the life lessons his show embodied and his ability to make each child feel he was speaking only to them. I said, "Thank you, Mr. Rogers, for being that special someone to all children, but especially to those who need the extra love."

In a moment I will always treasure, Mr. Rogers smiled and quietly replied, "And thank you for being that special someone to children also, and for the very important work you do." That sentiment stuck with me throughout my 33-year career in teaching, and it made me an even bigger Fred Rogers fan.

ANN HEISER · MOHRSVILLE, PA

Fred Rogers was the beloved host of *Mister Rogers' Neighborhood* from 1968 to 2001.

LEFT: FOTOS INTERNATIONAL/GETTY IMAGES

Friends in work and play, Bob and Dick entertained troops and enjoyed each other's company.

Thanks for the Memories, Bob

Touring with the legendary funnyman
left a lifelong impression.

An acrobat and trampoline artist operating under the stage name Dick Albers, I was a supporting act for Bob Hope on many of his domestic tours. In 1968, he asked me to be part of his show in Vietnam. In fact, we had such a good rapport that he chose me to be his seatmate on the long flight to and from Southeast Asia. We joked and laughed together the entire trip.

Our friendship went beyond the stage. I golfed with Bob and visited with him at his lovely home in Toluca Lake, California. We exchanged Christmas cards for many years until he died in 2003.

Bob was such an important part of my life that I titled my autobiography *Someday You're Not*

Coming Down, from something he wrote in one of the books he gave me.

He was always writing funny messages or tossing out zingers that way. In a book he sent to my dad, Bob wrote, "Thanks for having your offspring."

He introduced me to an audience once with the quip, "Dick's jumping career started at the age of 2 weeks, courtesy of an open diaper pin."

During one of our golf games, I hit a particularly long drive, but I hit it with a bit of a slice. As the ball headed toward the refreshment stand, Bob shouted, "Dick just knocked down the snack bar!"

DICK ALBERSHARDT · ALTAMONTE SPRINGS, FL

British actor David McCallum signs a playbill for fans Linda and Larry.

Mission: Accomplished

A fan didn't miss second opportunity
to meet David McCallum.

Like many young girls, I was infatuated with a television star. My crush was on the character played by David McCallum on *The Man from U.N.C.L.E.*

Many years later, I was on a business trip to London when I went to a delightful comedy starring McCallum called *Run for Your Wife* at the Criterion Theatre. Since I was alone and not very comfortable being out in the evening, I high-tailed it back to my hotel after the play ended, but I kept the playbill from this 1987 production.

Fast-forward to 2013, when McCallum agreed to attend the 50th anniversary showing in Omaha, Nebraska, of *The Great Escape*, a movie in which he had a small part alongside stars Steve McQueen and Charles Bronson. McCallum quite graciously accepted the invitation to host the showing of the

movie at our local art museum. He addressed the audience and later spent plenty of time greeting people who wanted to thank him for coming, get autographs and say hello.

When it was my turn to greet him, I placed the *Run for Your Wife* playbill on the table and said, "I've waited a long time for this."

At first he looked a bit taken aback, but when he noticed the playbill from the '80s, he was surprised and delighted. We struck up a conversation, and he signed the playbill, as well as *The Great Escape* brochure my husband, Larry, was holding, and offered to take a picture with us.

We still enjoy watching him play Dr. Mallard on *NCIS*. And we continue to feel that David is a real charmer, and quite "ducky!"

LINDA GOMEZ · OMAHA, NE

Treasured Pen Marks History

At the Capitol, a crack young speller
meets a famous fellow Texan.

When I was 14, in 1959, I traveled to Washington, D.C., to compete in the Scripps National Spelling Bee. As the regional winner from Lubbock, Texas, I was invited to meet then-Sen. Lyndon B. Johnson, D-Texas, who was Senate majority leader at the time. He shook my hand and presented me with a pen that featured a miniature picture of Johnson inside the capsule and the inscription "Compliments of Lyndon B. Johnson, Your United States Senator."

I've often wondered if today's National Spelling Bee competitors get the kind of VIP treatment I enjoyed then. I met both Texas senators and had lunch with Lubbock's congressman, George Mahon. I toured the White House, Bureau of Engraving, Andrews Air Force Base and FBI headquarters, and took a trip down the Potomac River to Mount Vernon. The spelling bee was held at the historic Mayflower Hotel; I've gone back many times over the years, reliving the excitement of that first memorable visit. Though I didn't win—I placed 12th out of 70 spellers—I remember the tournament and all its related events quite fondly.

Most of all, more than 60 years later, I still treasure that pen from LBJ. I've never seen another one like it. It's a special memento of a wonderful time in my life from a man who later became the president of the United States.

DAVID NELSON · HOUSTON, TX

He didn't know it, but David was meeting a future president on his trip to Washington for a spelling bee in 1959.

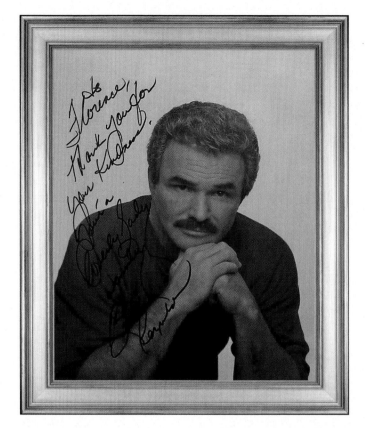

A box-office star in the '70s, Reynolds got his start in TV, a medium to which he returned throughout his long career.

Technician Produces Burt Reynolds Film

She could see that his heart was in the right place.

Coeur d'Alene, Idaho, is a beautiful area and draws celebrities who want to live here. In 1995 I was working as a medical technologist for four doctors at Family Health Associates, where I ran the lab and X-ray departments. One of our patients was actress Patty Duke, who was working on a TV show called *Amazing Grace*, in which she played a pastor. The show was being shot on location in Coeur d'Alene, and Duke, who also served as a co-producer, had Burt Reynolds as a guest actor for one of the episodes.

For the show's insurance purposes, Reynolds had to have an X-ray taken. He arrived at the clinic accompanied by two bodyguards. My department was near the front of the clinic—first door to the left—and the bodyguards waited there while Reynolds got his X-ray. He came into the room with me, and I had him take off his shirt. Next I measured his chest and had him put a gown on.

I took the X-ray, then Reynolds waited while I developed the film and had the doctor read it. When we were finished, Reynolds put his shirt on and gave me a peck on the cheek!

My husband was also in the lab, working on a piece of equipment, and he got to meet Reynolds. I remember that he complimented my husband's western shirt, which was from a store on the Indian reservation in Blackfoot, Idaho.

When Reynolds and his bodyguards left, he gave me an autographed picture. It says: "To Florence, Thank you for your kindness. You're a lovely lady. Warmly, Burt Reynolds."

And, yes, I did wash my face later that day.

FLORENCE STOVALL · HAYDEN, ID

Racing Form

The three young stars of *National Velvet* (1944),
Mickey Rooney (at top), Elizabeth Taylor and Jackie Jenkins,
pose in this studio shot. The film's story of a girl who rides in
Britain's Grand National horse race was Taylor's breakout role.

CHAPTER 10

....

HOLIDAYS AND CELEBRATIONS

When celebrating special occasions,
gathering with loved ones makes it all the
more magical.

Plaid-itude

I took this picture of my boyfriend and future husband, Scott Hintz, one fall in the 1980s. He was always goofing around. Here he's posing with a Halloween scarecrow in his front yard in Shantytown, Wisconsin.

LYNN HINTZ • ALMOND, WI

Barn Dance Memories

It all started out perfectly, but she couldn't plan for what happened next.

I spent weeks preparing for my birthday party in the fall of 1962. I was finally becoming a teenager! My first challenge was to convince Mom and Dad to let me invite both boys and girls to my party. They were apprehensive, but I argued that as a high school freshman, I was definitely old enough. It wasn't my fault I had skipped a grade and was a year younger than all my classmates.

Once my parents finally agreed, I began to look for the perfect venue, and found it at a relative's farm, 12 miles from my hometown of Beloit. I could use the hayloft, but I had to clean it out. It was hard and dirty work, yet the hours went by quickly as I thought of the fun ahead. The next obstacle was how to get everyone out to the farm, but I had a plan for that, too: a hayride.

Finally the big day came! Forty excited teens clambered onto two large hay wagons that my dad pulled with a tractor. My mom followed in the station wagon as we slowly headed to my birthday barn dance.

The party was even more glorious than I hoped. Everyone was having loads of fun dancing and gorging on cake and pop. The presents from my friends were all the things any teenage girl could want—lots of 45s and stuffed animals. Too soon it came to an end, and we loaded up the wagons to head back to town. We all looked forward to the ride home in the dark. I had a special guy to sit with, and all was silent and peaceful—until half a mile from town. There was a sudden scream. A boy had fallen off.

Pat had been sitting with his legs dangling over the edge of the wagon when his shoelace caught in a wheel. The wagon ran over his legs, but he didn't seem too badly hurt. Still, Mom took him to the hospital.

The mood was more somber as we started off again, and we no longer had Mom's headlights to see by. We were just a few minutes along when my 15-year-old brother, Mike, decided to move from the rear wagon to the front one. But it was so dark he misstepped and fell between the wagons, and he got caught on the hitch. When Dad stopped the tractor, Mike had been dragged several feet.

We rushed him to the emergency room, and then he was transferred to a hospital in Wichita, 170 miles away. A medical team there operated on his broken leg, inserting a steel rod to hold the bone together. It mended well and Mike was fine in a few months. However, my best party ever had turned into an unlucky bout of double bad luck that I will never forget!

JUDITH SIMMONS LYNCH · MANHATTAN, KS

HAPPY BIRTHDAYS

THE PERFECT CAKE
In July 1969, my mom, Mira, threw me a party about a month before I turned 5. We were about to move from Florida to Georgia, so it was the last get-together I had with my friends. The cake was memorable—a lot of frosting and a stunning topper of a horse-drawn white carriage. I wish I still had it! I'm the one smiling at the center back of this picture.
CHRISTINA SPALATIN
WAUWATOSA, WI

ALL SMILES
My uncle Zane Torrence stands next to the seven-layer cake his father, my grandpa, made for him in 1942 in honor of Zane's seventh birthday. As my dad's family was often strapped for money, I am sure this was a best-birthday-ever moment for Zane. The back of the photo notes "23 people enjoyed part of the cake that day."
DAWN TORRENCE · PERU, IN

ICE CREAM DREAMS
On my 10th birthday, Dad took me and my best friend, Jeanette, out for ice cream, a carnival, bowling and then ice cream—again! Back home we had cake and presents.
CHERYL MORGAN · BROOKLYN PARK, MN

PERFECT PARTIES

ALL DOLLED UP

When I turned 7 in July 1955, my mom let me invite both second grade classes of girls to a party—16 in all. It was a doll party: We all brought our dolls, and Mom made little ribbon prizes for each one. I'm fifth from left in the back row.
KATHLEEN HEAD McDONALD · ERIE, PA

A MAGICAL CAKE

When I turned 4, Mother invited my closest friends to a dress-up party. We gasped in amazement when she brought out the fabulous doll cake she'd made. It was pure magic.
LYNN ADKINS MOREAU · RICHMOND, VA

BUYING THE PARTY A COKE

For my 16th birthday, in 1961, my parents let me have a slumber party. My biggest memory by far is of my dad buying a whole case of Coke for the occasion. Pictured are Pat Rauschl, me and Sandy Peroutka.
SHIRLEY CHELLBERG CHANDLER
WAUSAU, WI

Iris turned 18 aboard a Canadian cruise liner en route to Niagara Falls.

Trip of a Lifetime

She celebrated with fellow graduates and a crew of thoughtful shipmates.

O f the many birthdays I've had in my life—almost 90 of them—one stands far and above the rest.

This birthday was in May 1949, the year I graduated from high school in New Madison, Michigan. Our school had 19 graduates that year, and we all went on a trip to Detroit.

From there, we were to travel by overnight cruise ship to Niagara Falls. For a small group of students from a rural school, it was the greatest adventure any of us could imagine.

We had two drivers who took us to Detroit, student Wilson Bunger and our senior adviser, Mr. Wendrick. On board we were two to a cabin. After settling in, we explored the ship.

I'll never forget the name: SS *Noronic* of Port Arthur, Ontario. A luxury liner known as "the queen of the Great Lakes," the *Noronic* could accommodate over 500 passengers.

The first night out we had dinner and a dance. At one point during the festivities, it was announced that a student was celebrating a birthday. I heard my name called and I was asked to come forward. Then all of the passengers and crew sang "Happy Birthday" to me. That moment is forever etched in my memory.

Our trip to visit the falls was magical. We saw the rapids, walked along the international bridge and then had lunch in the city before returning to Detroit the following day.

I have never forgotten that birthday. By 2019, when we would have celebrated our 70th reunion, only a few classmates were living.

There is a tragic postscript to the story of the *Noronic*: In the early hours of Sept. 17, 1949, four months after our trip, the ship caught fire while docked in Toronto, Ontario, with many lives lost.

Learning about the SS *Noronic*'s unfortunate fate makes my memory of her, when she was host to one of the happiest days of my life, all the more precious.

IRIS ROSS · CELINA, OH

Will You Be Mine?

Classmates of Luella Kern Robinson in Oelwein, IA,
exchanged valentines at school in the 1920s. Luella's
daughter, Sharon Robinson Spalding of Ashland, OR,
saved these little cards with their sentiments of friendship.

Don't jump at me.

To My Valentine

DON'T JUMP AT ME
German mechanical cards
had paper levers and
movable parts. This card
is supported by a stand
on the back; the stable
door folds open and the
pony and rider spring out.

WHITNEY MADE

Most cards in this collection are from the George C. Whitney Co., whose dainty designs were long popular with schoolchildren.

George Whitney took over his brother's stationery business, located in Worcester, MA, after he returned from serving on the Union side in the Civil War. Working with his brother Edward, he renamed the firm the Whitney Valentine Co. and bought up many competitors. By the turn of the century, over 90% of the valentines sold in the U.S. came from Worcester printers, most of which belonged to Whitney.

In January 1910, a fire, fueled by celluloid, paper and paint, destroyed part of the business. Luckily, that year's valentines had shipped; Easter novelties burned, but the company overcame what could have been utterly disastrous.

The family-run firm kept making valentines until 1942, when severe paper shortages during World War II forced the company to close.

Here, cards bearing the logo "Whitney Made" shine with bright lithography, delicate gold leaf and finely drawn illustrations, a contrast to the heavy paper of the pop-up stable, made in Germany (far left). Dates on these vintage cards range from 1924 to '27.

NATALIE WYSONG

By 1967, the five Silvers girls had two little brothers. Clockwise from lower right: Gena, holding Gary; Patti, Randy, Jackie, Ann and Becky.

Values, and Dresses, Are Made to Hand Down

Sewing five Easter frocks is a project in patience.

O ne by one, our mother, Mary Alice, called us five little girls to be measured. We had to hold our arms straight out from our sides as she slipped the tape around our chests and across our shoulders. She was making Easter dresses, and she had less than a week to finish!

She jotted down our measurements, then set the project aside to give us our baths and make supper. We gathered around for a Bible story, knelt to send childish petitions heavenward, and at last wriggled into the just-a-little-bigger-than-twin-size bed all five of us—ages 2 to 8—shared.

Our lullaby that night was the steady crunch, crunch, crunch of Mother's steel scissors against the tabletop. She drew the simple design and cut patterns from the *Cleveland Daily Banner*. Each seersucker dress was a different spring color, and starting with the smallest, each dress was a little larger than the one before. For her, there would be a maternity smock; the first of our two baby brothers was due to arrive in August.

A good tailor knows the importance of thread, and Mother took a spool from the row of Coats & Clark colors in her sewing box, unwound the sturdy strand, and gave it a tug. It needed to be strong enough to hold through summers to come as the dresses were handed down from Gena to Becky to me to Jackie and, at last, to Patti.

The next morning, our breakfast was cleared to make room for the heirloom Singer. And sing it did, giving a concert until finally, on Saturday, the last dress was sewn. Mother worked late finishing the hems by hand.

At church the next morning, we lined up beside her on the pew in the soft puffs of color. This was a special day, and it was the perfect occasion to wear dresses that were clean and new. We heard the remarkable Easter story of a love great enough to forgive us and to enable us to forgive and love each other. It was the same story that Mother patiently taught us every day.

ANN PORTER · OLD FORT, TN

Walking with the prizewinning cart are Elaine Heath, Betty Drudik, and Leonard and Mike Jedlicka. Seated are Gerald Jedlicka and Beverly York.

LABOR OF LOVE

MY MOTHER ALLOWED SOME OF HER
13 children to walk in a Labor Day parade in 1954. A farm family of Czechoslovakian descent, we felt quite honored to be part of the parade in Schuyler, Nebraska.

My dad and two of my brothers made the cart, which we knew would be very useful on our farm. We added goldenrods on the tires, signifying our love for the Nebraska flower. Mother sewed pretty ruffles onto the bottoms of our skirts, and she used peach basket covers to create the best hats in all of the parade. She allowed my brothers to wear their Sunday best, and she carefully hand-lettered the sign for the front of the cart—"Children, Our Most Important Crop."

We were so curious to see how the city folk organized and directed the local parade—the sight of the floats, bands, fire engines and horses was an unusual one for us hardworking farm kids.

Our cart won first place in the Kiddies' Division, and with the $10 prize we went to the Dairy Queen for ice cream cones.

ELAINE HEATH · OMAHA, NE

A FASHIONABLE EVENT
My husband and I dressed our four kids to the nines for my grandparents' golden anniversary banquet in Los Angeles in 1960.
JOANN SCHUELLER COOKE
PRESCOTT, AZ

Santa's Last Visit

A girl on the cusp of adolescence
receives a rare gift—wisdom.

E Even though I was 11, and long past the age of believing that Santa Claus would come flying in on a sleigh pulled by eight tiny reindeer, I still hoped for a Christmas morning surprise from him. In 1944, the country was at war in Europe and Asia. There were certainly more important things for me and my family to think about—but I was focused on my Christmas surprise.

Each year, I uncovered great things hidden in the back corners and top shelves of the dark hall closet. My annual investigations revealed that these were the same things that would magically appear under the tree as gifts on Christmas morning. So, in truth, I was seldom surprised when Christmas came—I'd seen all the presents in the closet. Still, I can say that at least I awaited them eagerly.

But despite a thorough search that year, I'd found nothing in the closet, so I began to worry that there would be no gifts at all for me. I could hardly believe it! I couldn't imagine giving up such a special event.

My friend Mary Anne was visiting on Christmas Eve and had a long talk with my mother. She and my mother often had long adult conversations in which I did not participate, being preoccupied with my own childish interests. Mary Anne was older, wiser and more mature than I was. She confirmed my suspicions after chatting with my mother; there would be no Christmas surprise for me, she said. My parents felt I'd outgrown a visit from Santa.

At bedtime, when my mother came in to wish me good night, I told her how upset I was that I would have nothing from Santa. (Of course, she already knew about my closet searches—parents always know more than their children think.)

"Honey, I'm so sorry," she said. "I didn't know that would still mean so much to you."

My father worked at the local refinery for many years, with changing shifts each week. That Christmas Day he'd left for a morning shift long before I got up.

So there I was, huddled in front of the gas stove, downing Christmas candy, fruit and nuts, sulking and having a serious pity party for myself. Just then, my brother Rod came in.

"A man in a red suit left this on the porch for you," he said.

He handed me a package wrapped in beautiful paper with a large red bow. My Santa surprise had somehow arrived after all! Inside was a marvelous thing, a treasure I'd never dreamed of having for my very own: a silver music box. I broke down in tears, suddenly ashamed of my selfishness.

Later, I found out what had happened. After my father arrived at work, he called the owner of Corner Drug, Mr. Bilberry, and arranged for him to deliver my present—even though the store was closed for the holiday. That Mr. Bilberry agreed is a perfect example of small-town caring. He and all of the townspeople were our friends, willing to go out of their way to help and bring joy to others.

Growing up, we children took this community for granted, never realizing what an amazing gift it was. Our parents taught us that the true spirit of Christmas is love, and it came to me in vivid color on that special Christmas morning.

Today, the music box sits on my dresser, where I see it each day and remember its special place in my heart. Its sweet song ends on a funny off-key note—the result of Daddy and me opening it once to see how it played. One piece of the mechanism was damaged during the operation.

Somehow that off-key note makes the music box feel even dearer to me.

There was never to be another Christmas when I expected a visit from Santa Claus. There was no need, since I had learned well the message of the season—love, given freely and unconditionally to me by my parents.

ANNE PALMER · HOUSTON, TX

Winging It

A Navy pilot devises a tactical plan
to get back home for Christmas.

During the 1980s, while our son Kevin was in the Navy, we considered ourselves fortunate that, with very few exceptions, we could spend Christmas with him most years.

One year, though, he came home around Dec. 15, saying it was the best he could get—Christmas Day leave was out of the question for him this year. So we celebrated the holiday early, complete with a tree and gifts, and Kevin returned to his base a couple of days later.

Yet as Christmas Eve neared, who should show up but Kevin, ready to celebrate Christmas for the second time that year, having somehow received more time off. Of course, we were delighted, and we rushed around to find a few last-minute gifts to exchange on the holiday. But the best gift was having Kevin home again.

It was a lucky break that kept our streak alive. We knew our run of good luck couldn't last, so we were grateful while it did.

In fact, a few years later, we were sure the streak had ended when Kevin, during his Thanksgiving leave, said that there was no way he'd be able to make it home for Christmas. His ship, the aircraft carrier USS *Ranger* CV 61, would be at sea until after New Year's Day.

So my wife, Catherine, and I had no plans for Christmas that year other than to sleep in and enjoy a quiet holiday at home.

Then on the morning of Christmas Eve, we heard a knock at the front door.

It can't be Kevin, we thought. We ignored the knocking, hoping whoever it was would go away. But the caller was persistent.

Finally, Catherine couldn't stand it anymore and got up to answer the door. The next thing I heard were shouts of joy and surprise, which could mean only one thing: It *was* Kevin. How could this be?

It turned out that our son had come up with a clever strategy on the spur of the moment. His job gave him access to details about the *Ranger*'s position on any given day. When he saw the ship's schedule, he realized he might be able to manage a trip home, so he asked for and was granted Christmas leave.

His shipmates, meanwhile, made fun of him for requesting time off at Christmas when their vessel would be somewhere in the middle of the Pacific Ocean over the holiday. But Kevin knew something they didn't.

With Christmas approaching, Kevin guessed there would be an overabundance of mail for the almost 4,000 crew members aboard the *Ranger*— and getting that mail would be crucial to the crew's morale. So, Kevin volunteered to retrieve the mail at the fleet post office in Hawaii. But the ship's position relative to Honolulu meant it was out of range of the usual mail-run aircraft, which was a Grumman C-2 Greyhound.

However, Kevin flew S-3 Vikings, which have a greater range than Grummans. With another Viking pilot, he flew to Hawaii and they loaded the jet with the crew's Christmas letters and packages until it looked for all the world like a modern Santa's sleigh.

Kevin handed the Viking's keys to the other pilot to take the presents to the ship, then headed to the airport to start his leave with a commercial flight to New York to spend the holiday with us.

A few years ago, our son retired from the Navy with the rank of commander. I like to think it was Kevin's skill at creative planning that gave him an advantage in his military career.

JIM GALLAGHER · RONKONKOMA, NY

ILLUSTRATIONS: MARYKATE MCDEVITT

Patrick Murphy took a midnight flight home for Christmas; the next year he was in Vietnam.

First-Class Christmas
A soldier gets an unexpected gift of conversation.

One of my gifts after earning my degree from the University of South Dakota in 1969 was a draft notice.

I was 22 when I reported to Fort Lewis in Washington state for basic training in October. I didn't expect to be able to return home to Sioux Falls for Christmas, but then, with short notice, the Army decided to give us leave.

I couldn't get a flight until Christmas Eve at midnight. I was wearing my dress uniform and seated in coach on a Northwest Orient nonstop flight to Minneapolis.

A flight attendant about my age requested I follow her up to first class, where she offered any beverage and food of my choosing. The real gift that Christmas Eve was that she sat next to me for the entire flight, and we talked familiarly, as if we knew each other.

In March, I went to Vietnam for 14 months and served with several different infantry units. In my time there I survived a half-dozen close encounters and was thankful to return with everything intact.

The memory of the Christmas Eve flight the year before sustained me during my Christmas in 1970, which I spent in Tuy Hoa, Vietnam. I don't recall the flight attendant's name, but her genuine caring and friendship has given me one of my favorite Christmas memories. She displayed the true spirit of giving—just being herself with a lonely soldier.

PATRICK MURPHY · SIOUX FALLS, SD

TRADITIONAL GIFT EXCHANGE

Old standbys for Mom and Dad.

1947 »

Timeless Quality

Harvel, based in New York City, sold a variety of watches with Swiss workings, which was a premium standard. Judging by its prices here—the costliest is the $430 ladies' platinum, second from bottom—this now-defunct brand was aimed at the elite market later led by Rolex and Cartier.

« 1947

America's Most Wanted

This is one of several Parker ads featuring illustration by Boris Artzybasheff, an expat Russian whose highly detailed technique anticipated the hyperrealism movement of the late 20th century. His forward-looking style suited the Parker 51, prized for its innovation. The company sold more than 2.1 million in 1947.

As the days inched closer to Christmas, Ann (left) wondered if Mary would get better in time to share the usual wonder of the Christmas holiday.

A Christmas to Remember

In sickness and in health, sisters are inseparable.

M y sister, Mary, had an after-school doctor's appointment, and so I darted off the bus alone and let myself into the house at the start of the two-week Christmas vacation in 1981.

When my mom, Grace, and Mary came home, I greeted them with a peppy "Hi!"—but their faces were serious. "The doctor thinks I have asthma," Mary said. It was seven days before Christmas and we should have been shaking our presents and debating what Santa would leave in our stockings, but Mary was tired and coughing. On Christmas Eve, Mary wasn't any better, so my worried parents took her to the emergency room. "I'll be home for Christmas, Annie," she said. I hung on to her clammy hand and hoped.

That night I went to sleep without my first friend in the world. I wasn't excited about presents and stockings; flying solo, my holiday was ho-hum.

On Christmas morning, my parents convinced me that Santa Claus visits hospitals, too, so Mary would get something in her stocking. Without much excitement, I reached into my stocking to find a deck of cards, a candy cane, a dollar and some peppermint lip balm. Then, without warning, I was struck with a severe flu bug.

My dad, Dan, spent Christmas morning taking care of me, but I became dehydrated. And so back we went to the emergency room. I would have to spend the night in the hospital, too.

Mary and I were in separate wings of the building, but we yammered on the phone until we both got tired. I felt better that night knowing Mary was nearby, even if the hospital frightened me. I went home the next day, and Mary the day after that.

We unwrapped our presents on New Year's Day, but it took a bout of the holiday fever to make me realize that shiny presents mean nothing if you don't have your closest friend with you.

ANN GALLAGHER · ST. PAUL, MN

Lumberjacks for a Day

Friends take a whack at selling Christmas trees.

M y friend Bob Ruzicka had 16 acres of Christmas trees in Wild Rose, Wisconsin, that were too much work for him to cut and sell. My pal Fraland "Smokey" Campbell and I made a deal with Bob that we would do the work and split the profit with him.

We drove 150 miles to the tree farm—we all lived in Waukesha County—on a beautiful Saturday. We picked the best trees and marked them with red yarn so we could still see them in case of heavy snow.

The following Saturday we returned to the tree plantation in zero-degree weather and with snow on the ground. We cut the first five trees and had to stop. The chain saw we'd rented was very heavy, and we had to bend down and hold the saw level a few inches above the ground to cut through the trunks. It was easier to use a bow saw for the rest of the trees. We'd brought a cement culvert—also very heavy—to pull the trees through, which made them more compact for tying and stacking.

We hauled the first load of trees in the dark.

The A&W stand in Wild Rose was closed for the winter, and the parking lot seemed like the perfect spot to sell the trees. We set them up, but when we returned with our second load, someone had pushed a large tree through the window of the restaurant, a $50 repair on top of the cost of renting the lot.

On our third and final trip, it began to rain, which made the trees extremely heavy. Besides the work of unloading, we had to haul trees from the back of the lot to replace ones that had sold.

We both had other jobs back home, but we sold the trees whenever we could. We gave away some to people who couldn't afford them and donated a big one to the church.

In the end we didn't have much money to share three ways, but Smokey and I certainly had an unusual holiday work experience to remember.

PHILLIP RADCLIFFE · LARGO, FL

A truck to haul their Christmas cargo was one of the things Phillip, left, and Smokey, right, had to secure for their side job in 1963. Robert Campbell, center, lent them his.

The Griffin children, clockwise from left: Esther, Violet, Henry, Ruby, Gwen and baby Leona.

1910 Christmas Magic

Santa Claus delights two little girls.

My great-aunt Violet Richards wrote about her Christmas memories as a 10-year-old for a newspaper near Georgetown, Colorado. Her sister Ruby was my grandmother. —Janet McBride

We were a large family of five girls and a boy, and an older cousin, Willie Leverton, who was reared by our parents, Samuel and Ada Lampshire Griffin, after his parents died.

Christmas Eve in 1910 was crisp, nipping noses and chilling fingers in mittens as we made our way to a holiday program at our church. Popcorn and cranberry garlands, candy beads and tinsel were strung on the silver spruce that reached to the ceiling. Gold balls weighed down the branches, and colored candles were adjusted just so and then lit for the celebration. It was up to parents to bring gifts to put around the tree for their children.

Usually our parents gave us candy in a net bag, fruit, nuts and a small gift, while other parishioners went all out with tea sets, little tables and chairs, wind-up engines and toys of all sorts. We children would leave the program wondering why we didn't get gifts like that. We never complained to Mama and Papa; we blamed Santa Claus.

That night, Ruby and I waited patiently as the other children got their gifts. Two dolls were still high up in the tree. We held our breath as a man climbed a ladder and cut the string from the dolls. He carried a porcelain bisque doll in blue satin to Ruby, so I knew the doll in pink organdy was mine. We danced all the way home, clasping the dolls we named Margaret and Geraldine. We hung our long black stockings in the back of the old Cribben & Sexton stove, and we took our dolls to bed to dream of Christmas Day.

VIOLET RICHARDS · SILVER PLUME, CO

CHRISTMAS CHEER

MAKING A LIST

Like many kids, I eagerly awaited the Sears Wish Book each year. Here, I'm thumbing through the catalogue at our family home in Mount Pleasant, Michigan, in 1961.
MILT SKILLMAN

HE SEES YOU WHEN YOU'RE PRAYING

My siblings and I knew we had to show proper reverence for the Nativity scene, lest we incur the wrath of our parents or—worse—the disapproval of Santa Claus. It looks like we stayed in Santa's good graces in 1939. Pictured, from left, are Laurie, Mary Ann, Joann, me (Bob) and Dick.
ROBERT SHAW · MADEIRA BEACH, FL

257 4877

"What Would You Like for Christmas?"

Our children Kevin, Christopher and Donna visited Santa in 1970
in Buffalo, New York. In this photo, Donna is reaching out to
her brother to give him support.

DONALD JANKOWSKI · BENSALEM, PA